# More Praise for *A CEO FOR ALL SEASONS*

"This book will make you better at taking risks, making decisions, adapting to new situations, and always moving forward. It's a master class in how to lead at every stage of the journey."
—Peter Voser, former CEO of Royal Dutch Shell

"Lifesaving advice for making tough decisions every step of the way—from securing the role to gracefully exiting. I wish I had had the benefit of this remarkable treatise when I was leading Sony."
—Kaz Hirai, former CEO of Sony

"Staying on top year in and year out in the face of ever-increasing competition and a changing game is exceedingly difficult. *A CEO for All Seasons* is your personal coach and a playbook to help you thrive."
—Herbert Hainer, former CEO of Adidas

# A CEO FOR ALL SEASONS

## Mastering the Cycles of Leadership

**CAROLYN DEWAR,
SCOTT KELLER,
VIKRAM MALHOTRA,
and KURT STROVINK**

SCRIBNER

New York  Amsterdam/Antwerp  London  Toronto  Sydney/Melbourne  New Delhi

Scribner
An Imprint of Simon & Schuster, LLC
1230 Avenue of the Americas
New York, NY 10020

For more than 100 years, Simon & Schuster has championed authors and the stories they create. By respecting the copyright of an author's intellectual property, you enable Simon & Schuster and the author to continue publishing exceptional books for years to come. We thank you for supporting the author's copyright by purchasing an authorized edition of this book.

No amount of this book may be reproduced or stored in any format, nor may it be uploaded to any website, database, language-learning model, or other repository, retrieval, or artificial intelligence system without express permission. All rights reserved. Inquiries may be directed to Simon & Schuster, 1230 Avenue of the Americas, New York, NY 10020 or permissions@simonandschuster.com.

Copyright © 2025 by McKinsey & Company, Inc.

All rights reserved, including the right to reproduce this book or portions thereof in any form whatsoever. For information, address Scribner Subsidiary Rights Department, 1230 Avenue of the Americas, New York, NY 10020.

First Scribner hardcover edition October 2025

Simon & Schuster strongly believes in freedom of expression and stands against censorship in all its forms. For more information, visit BooksBelong.com.

SCRIBNER and design are trademarks of Simon & Schuster, LLC

For information about special discounts for bulk purchases, please contact Simon & Schuster Special Sales at 1-866-506-1949 or business@simonandschuster.com.

The Simon & Schuster Speakers Bureau can bring authors to your live event. For more information, or to book an event, contact the Simon & Schuster Speakers Bureau at 1-866-248-3049 or visit our website at www.simonspeakers.com.

*Interior design by Jason Snyder*

Manufactured in the United States of America

1 3 5 7 9 10 8 6 4 2

Library of Congress Cataloging-in-Publication Data has been applied for.

ISBN 978-1-6680-9834-9
ISBN 978-1-6682-1257-8 (Int Exp)
ISBN 978-1-6680-9836-3 (ebook)

# CONTENTS

**INTRODUCTION**
The Four Seasons of a CEO ... 3

**CHAPTER ONE**
Stepping Up: Becoming a
High-Potential CEO Candidate ... 21

**CHAPTER TWO**
Starting Strong: Making Your CEO
Transition a Catalyst for Renewal ... 39

**CHAPTER THREE**
Staying Ahead: How the Best CEOs
Continually Improve Performance ... 57

**CHAPTER FOUR**
Sending It Forward: Successfully
Transitioning Out of the CEO Role ... 81

**CONCLUSION**
The Future of the CEO Role ... 97

**APPENDIX A**
Reflection Exercises ... 113

**APPENDIX B**
CEO Biographies ... 139

**ACKNOWLEDGMENTS** ... 187

**NOTES** ... 189

**INDEX** ... 193

**ABOUT McKINSEY & COMPANY** ... 205

# A CEO FOR ALL SEASONS

> *The seasons are what a symphony*
> *ought to be: Four perfect movements*
> *in harmony with each other.*
> —ARTHUR RUBINSTEIN

INTRODUCTION

# The Four Seasons of a CEO

The desire to divide experiences into beginnings, middles, and ends is entrenched in human nature. Whether it's the stories we tell, movies we watch, journeys we take, projects we complete, or even how we approach a typical day, month, or year, we see a clear progression from a starting point through a central phase to a final conclusion. We like to think in this way because it helps us manage complexity, makes planning easier, and allows us to take stock of our progress and to learn and adjust as we confront the unique challenges at each stage of the journey.

The journey of a CEO is no different. The role has a beginning, middle, and end, and the challenges leaders face early on are often far different than those midway through and near retirement. As senior partners at McKinsey & Company, a firm focused on helping the most senior leaders to have the highest possible impact, we've spent the vast majority of our careers counseling the CEOs of many of the world's largest and most iconic institutions. Doing so has made us acutely aware of the different cycles leaders and organizations pass through. For us, the most apt analogy to describe these cycles is the four seasons of the year.

1. **Spring: Preparing for the role (stepping up).** The two to three years before the board decides on the next CEO are when you should be gaining the experience, developing the skills, and demonstrating the qualities of an exceptional leader. Doing so will position you as a natural choice when the time comes and will prepare you to take the reins if you do get the job.

2. **Summer: Transitioning into the role (starting strong).** During your first two years in the CEO role, you need to get the organization to work at full potential productivity in the direction you've chosen. During this time, you should be taking bold actions that set the tone for your entire tenure.

3. **Fall: Navigating the middle years (staying ahead).** After starting strong, your next challenge will be to shape the company's long-term journey and combat complacency—both your own and that of your employees. This means creating successive "S-curves" (periods of intense activity and radical improvement) that will boost performance at every level: You as a leader, your team, and the organization as a whole.

4. **Winter: Transitioning out of the role (sending it forward).** In this final stage, you're preparing to hand over the reins to your successor. That process involves recognizing when to leave, navigating the transition gracefully, and discovering your next journey.

Thinking of the CEO leadership cycle as a series of seasons is instructive at both the individual and institutional level. Individually, a farmer prepares the land and plants crops in spring, grows them in the summer, harvests them in the fall, and prepares for the next planting by purchasing seed stock and maintaining equipment during winter. In the same way, what a CEO does in each season affects what happens in the next.

Farmers, however, don't just manage season to season. They look ahead many years to optimize crop rotation, pest management, biodiversity, and so on. Similarly, on an institutional level, each four-stage journey of a CEO is intrinsically connected to the journeys of the CEO who came before and of the one who will come after. For example, roughly 30 percent of what determines the success of a sitting CEO's tenure is driven by what the leader inherited from their predecessor (for example, company size, debt levels, and past R&D investments). Further, given that each CEO's "winter" dovetails with another's "spring," transferring knowledge across generations can be of great value. Simply put, organizations that have the institutional capability to cultivate high-potential CEO candidates, ramp them up successfully, and unlock their "S-curve" performance are far more likely to thrive over decades. This insight is extremely relevant to boards, which are the ultimate stewards of an organization's long-term performance.

Ultimately, the rhythm of the four seasons illuminates the long-term connection that exists between the CEO and the company they lead: The CEO's personal success is defined by whether they can successfully and regularly renew their institution. Those who grasp this larger perspective inherently see themselves as servant leaders, building their organizations with a view far beyond their own tenures to deliver the greatest long-term impact.

## The CEO's Almanac

As authors, we've already written in depth about how CEOs can excel in their roles—so why write more? The answer lies in our wanting to offer a more focused guide that spotlights how a CEO's tasks change over time. Carolyn, Scott, and Vik's *New York Times* best-selling book, *CEO Excellence: The Six Mindsets That Distinguish the Best Leaders from the Rest*, and Kurt's coauthored *The Journey of Leadership: How CEOs Learn to Lead from the Inside Out*, are both big-bite, comprehensive reference books for CEOs who want to master aspects of the job that loom large in *every* season. As we've continued to work with the most senior leaders in organizations, however, we've recognized the value of offering punchier, quick-hit advice that is more time-specific and speaks to what will matter most in each *separate* season—much like a farmer's almanac provides seasonal suggestions for its readers to optimize their annual cycles.

Our first task was to see if such a manual already exists. A survey of management literature revealed a range of resources available to CEOs. On one end of the spectrum are qualitative studies largely based on anecdotal evidence, and on the other are highly quantitative works that analyze the performance of thousands of CEOs to discern patterns. Looking at all of the available advice, however, we couldn't find anything that matched what we were hearing from CEOs that they really want:

- **To learn from those who've truly excelled in the role.** All of the research we've seen looks simply at the "average" experience of all CEOs. But who wants to be—or learn from—the average? We'd rather learn guitar playing from Jimi Hendrix, basketball from Caitlin Clark, or narration from David Attenborough than from an average performer. CEOs no doubt feel the same when it comes to learning how to be a great chief executive, and with good reason: Top-quintile CEOs create thirty times more economic value than the next three quintiles combined. Clearly, they think and do things differently than "the average." For our research, we specifically made sure to interview those CEOs who were the best at what they did based on rigorous criteria, even if securing interviews with these CEOs was more challenging.

- **To absorb content that's prescriptive, not just descriptive.** An article in the *Harvard Business Review* by former Harvard Business School dean Nitin Nohria titled "The CEO's Journey Is a 3-Act Play" argues that the likely missteps in a CEO's first act are assuming unanimous support from the board and being unprepared for the job's time demands. In Claudius Hildebrand and Robert Stark's *The Life Cycle of a CEO*, the authors conclude that CEOs enter a "sophomore slump" after year one and suffer stagnation in their middle years. All of that is good to know, but the real question is how to steer clear of such pitfalls. We're more interested in creating the equivalent of a thermostat (a practical tool that will help leaders achieve better outcomes) than a thermometer (a simple readout describing what is).

- **To find a "Goldilocks" format.** The articles we've read tend to promote concepts without enough practical examples to help apply them. Moreover, the books we've seen are padded with so many descriptions and lengthy stories that it's hard to distill the key points. To us, these overviews are the equivalent of the "too hot" and "too cold" bowls of porridge that failed to satisfy Goldilocks in the popular fairy tale. Hopefully, you'll find that this book is, by comparison, "just right"—short and conversational, but laden with insights on how to take action at every step.

Whether you're an aspiring senior leader or new-to-the-job CEO, we hope this is the hands-on guide you've been looking for. If you want to both flourish in the middle years of the role *and* have successors benefit from the strength of the organization you've left behind, this compendium is your best guide. And if you're a board member wanting to boost your company's performance across the lifespans of multiple CEOs, you'll find the essentials you need here. Further, as with *CEO Excellence*, our goal is not to help only the most senior leaders. All leadership roles have life cycles, and therefore we believe many of the lessons forged in the crucible of one of the most complex, challenging, dynamic, and high-impact leadership roles in the world will be applicable and invaluable to all leaders everywhere.

## Identifying the Best

To learn from the best, we knew it was essential to identify who they are. If you wanted to learn from the most consistently excellent athlete alive today, how would you go about determining who that is? You'd likely start by selecting a pool of seasoned, potential candidates. An all-star only in their second year, for example, wouldn't have enough of a track record to qualify for an all-time accolade. You'd then screen candidates according to some objective measures of performance, such as goals scored, points per game, championship titles, and so on. From there, you'd apply more subjective factors such as the athlete's mental toughness and behavior off the field. Last, you'd want to make sure everyone was being evaluated on a level playing field.

Our approach to determining the most consistently excellent CEOs was similar. We started with the list of leaders who've sat in the chief executive chair at the world's one thousand largest companies in the last fifteen years. There were more than two thousand of these individuals. We then selected those who had a tenure of six years or more. Our rationale was that this time frame allows for at least two years in each of the role's early, middle, and later stages. We further screened for "excess TRS"—the total financial return to shareholders in excess of the return industry peers have delivered (adjusted for geographical variations in growth). This left us with just under five hundred individuals who passed the tenure bar and performed clearly above the average.

From there, we took into account a set of additional factors: the individual's ethical conduct, employee sentiment, the company's environmental and societal impact, the strength of succession planning, and, in the cases of those who'd retired, whether the business continued to outperform financially in the years after they stepped down. These measures are already rigorously incorporated into many existing "best CEO" lists such as the *Harvard Business Review*'s Top 100 CEOs, *Barron's* Top 30 CEOs, *CEOWORLD*'s Most Influential CEOs, *Forbes*' America's 100 Most Innovative Leaders, and *Fortune*'s Most Powerful Women in Business. This brought our list down to 138 CEOs.

As a next step, we ensured there was an appropriate diversity of industries, genders, nationalities, and ownership structures by including excellent CEOs from outside the pool of the largest one thousand companies. (That said, all these CEOs still hail from large organizations that generate billions of dollars in revenue and/or have many thousands of employees.) We looked for CEOs who led remarkable transformations while delivering stronger results than their peers. This brought our list of CEOs up to a well-rounded total of two hundred leaders who can credibly be considered the best in the world in recent history. We estimate that the economic value created by this group of two hundred leaders is a stunning $5 trillion in excess of their peers. That's more than the annual gross domestic product of Germany, the world's third largest economy.

With this screening process, we essentially replicated the methodology used in *CEO Excellence*. A final step was needed, though. We wanted to see how this group fared against other CEOs across each year of their tenure. That way, we'd be able to answer whether these individuals typically perform better in *all four* seasons. The graph on the following page shows that the best CEOs don't experience a "sophomore slump" after year one, nor do they fall into a complacency trap during their middle years. Instead, year in and year out, they deliver above-market and above-industry returns to their shareholders.

Does the graph mean that these leaders didn't make mistakes along the way? They would be the first to admit that they most definitely did! What's remarkable, though, is that like a coach whose team might have lost a game to a lesser opponent early in the season but still qualified for the playoffs and won the championship, these CEOs were able to sense, learn, and act quickly so that they never endured a losing season. As with many high-achievers in other fields, those in business who achieve the most tend to be those who are the best at getting better. Sam Hazen, CEO of HCA Healthcare, describes how he keeps improving his performance: "I'm in my seventh year as CEO and despite our success, I still feel like I'm behind. That creates an internal motor for me to do more to make a difference for society, to benchmark our performance

## The Best CEOs Generate a Higher Shareholder Return Than Their Peers at Every Stage

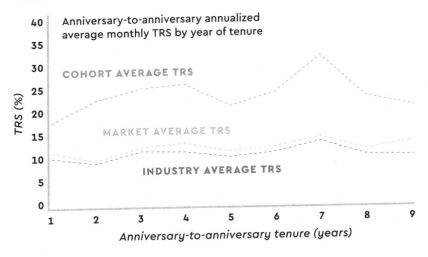

Anniversary-to-anniversary annualized average monthly TRS by year of tenure

against the best inside and outside of our industry, to structure my team better, and to continue my own development. It keeps the organization moving, and it keeps me moving."

Once we identified the best leaders, we interviewed as many as possible while mining related content from the vast body of research and interviews that we've amassed over the past five years. In the end, of the top two hundred CEOs whom we identified, we spoke to eighty-three.

We were excited to connect again with a number of CEOs whom we'd interviewed for *CEO Excellence*, such as JPMorgan Chase's (JPMC) Jamie Dimon, Adobe's Shantanu Narayen, and Westpac's Gail Kelly. We were also thrilled to interview a new group of exceptional leaders. Gail Boudreaux, one of *Forbes*' World's Most Powerful Women of 2024, gave us a master class in leading through the COVID-19 pandemic as CEO of the Fortune 20 insurer Elevance Health. Peter Wennink, CEO of the Netherlands-based semiconductor giant ASML, which is one of the world's most important technology companies in today's race for high-quality chips, explained how he earned his reputation for openness and approachability. Arvind Krishna, CEO of IBM, shed light on how he adapted his leadership approach to guide the global technology giant through transformations in AI, hybrid cloud, and quantum computing.

To get the most out of the conversations, we again used an interview technique that originated in clinical psychology known as laddering. It involves using various methods of inquiry, such as storytelling, asking provocative questions, posing hypotheticals, role-playing, and circling back to previous statements to uncover multiple levels of why someone holds a particular opinion and takes a specific action. This made for extremely interesting and intense discussions, which often lasted several hours and at times extended across multiple meetings.

## Illuminating the Blind Spots

To uncover what it takes to win in each season, we've combined three inputs. The first is our interviews across multiple exceptional CEOs, from which we can discern patterns as well as valuable tools and approaches. The second is research by others that describes what "average" looks like, which helps us understand what's different between the two groups. A third input is understanding where CEOs typically have "blind spots." These are the areas where chief executives, on average, tend to be "unconsciously unskilled"—that is, unaware of what they don't know.

We looked far and wide for insights on CEO blind spots and—not finding anything useful—we concluded it was up to us to do the research. To do so, we fielded a large-scale survey with a respondent pool that excluded executives from our top 200 list. We surveyed three groups: CEOs, their direct reports, and board members. Each group rated the CEO on how well he or she was delivering on best practices related to each of the six responsibilities of the CEO's role that we identified in *CEO Excellence*: setting direction, aligning the organization, mobilizing through leaders, engaging the board, connecting with stakeholders, and managing personal effectiveness. The specific questions we asked are in the table below.

## How Well Are You Fulfilling the Six Responsibilities of the CEO Role?

| DIRECTION SETTING: How well am I putting the "Be Bold" mindset into practice? | Not at all — Completely |
|---|---|
| **Vision:** Do we have a clear and compelling vision that reframes what winning looks like and that's owned by the whole enterprise? | ⊢—┼—┼—┼—┤ |
| **Strategy:** Have we created a short list of clearly defined big moves at the enterprise level that will distance us from our competitors? | ⊢—┼—┼—┼—┤ |
| **Resource allocation:** Are we "thinking like an outsider" to actively reallocate resources (e.g., dollars, people, and management attention) to our highest priorities, even when it's hard? | ⊢—┼—┼—┼—┤ |
| ORGANIZATION ALIGNMENT: How well am I putting the "Treat the Soft Stuff as the Hard Stuff" mindset into practice? | |
| **Culture:** Are we targeting specific areas of culture change to further unlock the execution of our strategy and pursuing those changes systematically? | ⊢—┼—┼—┼—┤ |
| **Organization design:** Is our organization characterized by a balance of stability and agility that minimizes friction in execution? | ⊢—┼—┼—┼—┤ |
| **Talent:** Are the most value-creating roles in our organization filled with the right talent, and do they have a strong leadership pipeline? | ⊢—┼—┼—┼—┤ |

| | Not at all | Completely |
|---|---|---|
| **LEADERSHIP MOBILIZATION:** How well am I putting the "Solve for the Team's Psychology" mindset into practice? | | |
| **Team composition:** Is my senior team the right size, comprised of people with complementary skills, and characterized by an "enterprise first" mindset? | ⊢——⊢——⊢——⊢——⊣ | |
| **Teamwork:** Does my senior team use data and dialogue effectively to make timely decisions on topics that "only the top team" can decide on? | ⊢——⊢——⊢——⊢——⊣ | |
| **Operating rhythm:** Does my senior team have an effective annual operating rhythm and business review cadence that drives execution and minimizes surprises? | ⊢——⊢——⊢——⊢——⊣ | |
| **BOARD ENGAGEMENT:** How well am I putting the "Help Directors Help the Business" mindset into practice? | | |
| **Relationships:** Have I built trust with my board members by being radically transparent and showing an interest in their views? | ⊢——⊢——⊢——⊢——⊣ | |
| **Capabilities:** Do we have the right profiles on the board and are we sufficiently educating directors and pulling them in to help where they can? | ⊢——⊢——⊢——⊢——⊣ | |
| **Board meetings:** Are board sessions well prepped, run effectively, and focused on the future (going well beyond fiduciary topics only)? | ⊢——⊢——⊢——⊢——⊣ | |
| **EXTERNAL STAKEHOLDER CONNECTION:** How well am I putting the "Start with 'Why?'" mindset into practice? | | |
| **Purpose:** Are we clear on the holistic impact we aspire to (our "why?"), and have we embedded that into the core of how we run our business? | ⊢——⊢——⊢——⊢——⊣ | |
| **Interactions:** Do we fully understand our stakeholders' needs (their "why?") and find constructive common ground with them? | ⊢——⊢——⊢——⊢——⊣ | |
| **Moments of truth:** Have we built resilience ahead of any potential crises such that we'll be able to mitigate their impact and use them to unlock opportunities? | ⊢——⊢——⊢——⊢——⊣ | |

| PERSONAL EFFECTIVENESS: How well am I putting the "Do What Only You Can Do" mindset into practice? | Not at all     Completely |
|---|---|
| **Time and energy:** Do I manage my time and energy well, and do I have the right office support in place to help me successfully and sustainably do what only I can do as the CEO? | ├──┼──┼──┼──┤ |
| **Leadership model:** Am I leading in a way that is authentic to my convictions and values while also adjusting my behaviors to what the organization needs? | ├──┼──┼──┼──┤ |
| **Perspective:** Do I approach my position with humility, focusing on helping others to succeed and continually improving my ability to do so? | ├──┼──┼──┼──┤ |

Our goal was to compare how the CEOs saw themselves versus how others perceived them. In analyzing the results, we recognized that perception (the way things are interpreted or understood) is not necessarily reality (the way things are). However, we felt it was reasonable to assume that areas where both the board and direct reports had a meaningfully different view than the CEO were highly likely to be genuine blind spots. (The chart on page 17 shows the survey's quantitative outcomes.)

What we found reminded us of radio host Garrison Keillor's description of the fictional Minnesota small town of Lake Wobegon, a place "where all the women are strong, all the men are good-looking, and all the children are above average." This human tendency to overestimate our own abilities, achievements, and performance has become known as the Lake Wobegon Effect.

CEOs, on average, seem to be inhabitants of Lake Wobegon. Regardless of tenure, they score themselves higher than direct reports score them 100 percent of the time, and higher than boards score them 80 percent of the time. The 20 percent of time that the board is more bullish than the CEO tends to be in the leader's early tenure—which makes sense given that the board is undoubtedly optimistic about their CEO choice; meanwhile, the CEO is still learning the role and therefore not yet feeling totally confident.

That said, as we looked into blind spots in each season, we found that in the early years new CEOs tend to be most overconfident about their ability to shift the culture. They typically come into the role with a clear point of view on where the organization needs to go, yet underestimate the difficulty of aligning and mobilizing the employees to get there. This reinforces one of our findings from *CEO Excellence*, which is that the soft stuff—influencing behavior change at scale—is the hard stuff, especially when getting started.

New CEOs also feel overconfident in terms of how well they're managing their personal effectiveness. It often takes more time than they anticipate to balance being who they want to be with who the *organization* needs them to be in the role. Their time and energy also become fragmented in ways that take away from successfully and sustainably doing what only they can do as the CEO. Adena Friedman, CEO of Nasdaq, a leading global technology company serving the financial system, confesses: "At the end of that first year, I looked at everything I'd done—how many speaking engagements, how many client meetings, how many trips, et cetera—and I realized I was sprinting a marathon." Fortunately, by recognizing this early, she was able to adjust accordingly.

In the middle years, a blind spot often emerges related to having a clear and compelling vision for the company. This is because once a leader's initial set of bold moves has largely played out positively (if the moves haven't, the CEO is likely on their way out—involuntarily), their intense focus on a clear "North Star" dissipates. Without the inspiration, boldness, and mandate for change that CEOs feel early in their tenure, they find it hard to press "reset." Over time, observes IBM's Krishna, "people get hung up on the success of old strategies, and then they refuse to acknowledge that times have changed, and new strategies are needed." Similarly, at this stage, maintaining perspective and remaining open to new ideas can become an issue. As the author of the organization's journey to this point, the CEO tends to feel like they have all the answers.

During the latter years of a CEO's tenure, strategic clarity becomes an issue. For some, this can be the result of a desire to protect one's legacy by preventing any potential late-in-the-game ball drops, especially as it relates to hitting near-term earnings targets. Others may make overly risky moves to avoid a growth slowdown or to relieve boredom. Teamwork can also suffer, often because the CEO has undermanaged the dynamics of the succession process, allowing potential candidates to jockey for position and lower performers to recognize they won't likely survive the transition.

The chart below summarizes the predominant blind spots at each stage of the journey.

## CEO Blind Spots Change Over Time

▶ *CEO self ratings versus others on a scale of 1–5*

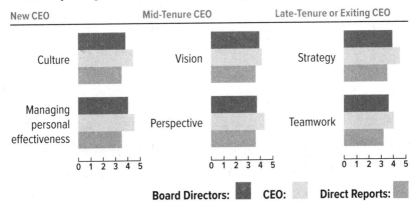

With this more nuanced understanding of the pitfalls CEOs are likely to stumble into as they navigate each stage of the journey, we were well positioned to ask the right, high-impact questions to those top-performing CEOs who'd mostly avoided them. This, we felt, was a path to providing the most insightful guidance.

Somewhat unexpectedly, we couldn't help but conclude that the blind spots assessment we describe on pages 13–15 can be an invaluable tool to help CEOs avoid falling victim to blind spots. Do you, as a leader, have a handle on where you stand on each relevant practice among the six responsibilities listed? If your answer is "yes," but you haven't actually asked your direct reports and board members for feedback, our research suggests your answer is very likely coming from Lake Wobegon!

We encourage you to use this tool since doing so reflects a best practice of great CEOs. As we've described, these leaders aren't without their own setbacks and blind spots, but they're quick to identify and correct them, and they use the broader environment and their teams to adjust, innovate, and out-compete. Doug Peterson, the former CEO of S&P Global, puts it this way: "From day one you need to have the mentality of always learning, growing, improving, and being very objective about who you are and what you are."

---

Being a CEO for all seasons matters not just for the individual and the institution, but for society at large. The decisions that chief executives make fuel economies and directly affect the lives of their employees (over 70 million people work for the world's 2,000 largest companies alone).

And it should go without saying that CEOs have significant environmental, social, ethical, and political impact. In this book, we share everything we've learned from the very best of the best to help you excel in whatever leadership season you happen to find yourself in, and to lay the groundwork for successful seasons to come.

> *It is not the mountain we conquer but ourselves.*
> —SIR EDMUND HILLARY

CHAPTER ONE

# Stepping Up: Becoming a High-Potential CEO Candidate

The world's highest peak is Mount Everest, majestically rising almost 30,000 feet above sea level. Many mountaineers spend years training and preparing to make the trek, yet few make it to the top. Since Edmund Hillary and Tenzing Norgay first reached the mountain's summit in 1953, only about seven thousand people have followed.

The challenges of the climb multiply the closer one gets to the top. The trail from the final camp to the summit is dubbed "the death zone," where thin air and brutal weather combine to create confusion and hallucinations among climbers, as well as a host of health-related challenges. For the select few who make it through, though, there is the magical feeling of standing, literally, on top of the world.

Since the 1950s, fewer people have made it to the top of Fortune 500 companies than have scaled Mount Everest. When Mary Barra joined General Motors as an eighteen-year-old engineering intern, the odds that she'd someday sit in the CEO chair were far less than one in 750,000 (the number of General Motors employees at the time). It was more probable that she'd be struck by lightning! Yet today, she's more than ten years into her tenure as the first woman ever to lead a US automaker.

Barra's journey to the top, like that of most Fortune 500 CEOs, involved continuous learning and compiling a record of success across a wide variety of increasingly senior positions. During her career, she honed many vital leadership traits, such as strategic thinking, relationship building, risk taking, authenticity, humility, objectivity, resilience, stamina, and decisiveness. A few years before becoming CEO, however, she suddenly felt sidetracked when she was unexpectedly shifted to HR—the type of soft job that has long been a way station for women finishing out their careers.

As Barra learned, any leader two or three years out from the top job faces a final ascent as fraught with challenges as the one on Mount Everest. Some executives find themselves sidelined. Others become part of the top team only to discover that they have no desire to step up further. Still others become disoriented, lose their balance, and fall. For some, external factors (e.g., political, technological, competitive) interrupt the path to becoming the CEO—at least at their company. "You can dedicate the first thirty years of your career to working your way up the ladder, hoping that when the game of thrones happens, all of the luck and skill comes together at the same moment," says Etsy's CEO Josh Silverman, "but so many things need to come together to succeed."[1]

While there is no way to guarantee success, if you're a senior executive who aspires to the top job, the following advice will greatly increase your odds:

- Gut check your motivations and expectations
- Elevate your perspective while boldly delivering results
- Round out your profile with humility
- Understand the CEO selection process and put your best foot forward

## Gut Check Your Motivations and Expectations

"Everest is not about summiting, adding to your image, the conquest of nature or of other humans," experienced mountaineers share in a guide to climbing Mount Everest.[2] To climbers driven by such motivations, these mountaineers say, "You will become a prisoner of other people's judgment in your desire of proving self-worth. You will climb blinded and feel an immense failure if not summiting. Or if successful—go home, celebrate your triumph and fame, and, when the lights eventually are turned toward someone else, end up empty." Former Cincinnati Children's Hospital Medical Center (CCHMC) CEO Michael Fisher makes a similar point when it comes to leading organizations: "If the main reason you want to have the CEO title is for ego, that's unlikely to be a sustainable motivator over time."

At the same time, there are many climbers on the mountain whose fear of failure is overwhelming, which can lead to catastrophe if they attempt to summit. As former Medtronic CEO and Harvard Business School professor Bill George shares, "A lot of CEOs who get in the role don't step up. 'I could lose my job,' they say to themselves. If you aren't willing to put your job on the line, you shouldn't be the CEO." In George's observation, "I find a number of very well qualified people aren't good CEOs. They don't have the courage."

The table on the next page provides an initial litmus test for whether you've got the right mindset to succeed in the top role. If your honest answers fall into the "self-oriented mindset" category, chances are your motivations are too ego-driven, and you're not a good fit. The ego satisfaction you'll get from landing the top job will soon provide small comfort in the face of mounting demands. If your answers land in the "self-critical mindset" category, it's likely you don't have the confidence to succeed. Your greatest fears will quickly materialize as you hesitate, fail to spin all the plates needed, and then see one or more fall.

## Do You Really Want to Be a CEO?

|  | Self-Oriented mindset | Self-Critical mindset | Sustainable mindset |
|---|---|---|---|
| **Why I want to be CEO** | It's my natural next step and comes with more power, money, and esteem | I'm not sure I do—I'm not 100% CEO-ready and don't want to not do a good job | I have an exciting vision for the impact the company and I can acheive together |
| **What being chosen as CEO would mean** | I've proven myself, attained my ultimate goal, and have the recognition I deserve | Others have confidence in me that I can do the job | It would be a privilege to serve as CEO for the company's next chapter |
| **What not being chosen as CEO would mean** | I lost the race and am embarrassed that I didn't get chosen | I was right, I don't have what it takes to lead at the next level | I'll continue becoming the best leader I can be, whether here or elsewhere |
| **How I'll add value as CEO** | I'll be able to solve the tough problems that no one else can | I'll work as hard as I can so that I won't let others down | I'll ask the tough questions and make decisions that unlock the full potential of others |
| **How I'll feel as CEO** | I'll feel like I'm in the center of the action, with other people around me to help | I'll have "imposter syndrome" and hope no one realizes I'm not ready | I'll feel lonely because of my vantage point and need for objectivity |
| **How I'll act as CEO** | I'll be the boss and can run the place the way I want with confidence | I'll surround myself with great people and empower them to lead | I'll do the work that only I can do as CEO with both confidence and humility |

If the sustainable mindsets ring true to you, you will be predisposed to handle the aforementioned six demands of the job we identified in *CEO Excellence*: setting the direction, aligning the organization, mobilizing leaders, engaging the board, connecting with stakeholders, and managing your personal effectiveness.

Even with the right mindset, however, it's important to be clear-eyed about the intensity of the role. "There's more things to do than you have time for," says IBM's Arvind Krishna. "You need to wake up to the fact that you have to give up certain things in your personal life." Doug Peterson, former CEO of S&P Global, affirms, "These jobs aren't for everybody. The travel alone can take its toll. It's important that people are honest with themselves about what they want to do." Many CEOs secretly agree that the best job in the world is actually the one right below the CEO. There the spotlight is less glaring, yet the opportunities to make a difference are great, as are the rewards.

For these reasons, we encourage any executive setting their sights on the summit to do some genuine soul-searching before deciding to make the final ascent. If it's all about you, or if you're doing it out of a sense of obligation, know that the top will be a hostile, extreme place where no one will rescue you during times of trouble. As CCHMC's Fisher puts it, "If you're not driven by a deep care and concern for the institution you have the privilege to lead and for its stakeholders, then when the going gets tough, you won't step up to the challenge." If, however, you're driven by a passion and vision for how you can help others climb further and faster to achieve new heights collectively, you'll more than likely end up on a deeply fulfilling adventure." ASML's Peter Wennink captures this winning mindset: "Nobody on the team is more important than what we're trying to do together. Nobody, not even the CEO."

Last, when gut checking your motivations and expectations, don't forget to consider the impact that the new job will have on your family members. PepsiCo's Ramon Laguarta advises, "If you have a weak relationship, being the CEO will kill it for sure. But if you have a strong relationship, you don't want to jeopardize it for the job." To manage this dynamic, it's important to have conversations up front with your family, if you have one. "I can tell you our daughters were not thrilled at all. They hated it," former General Mills CEO Ken Powell explains. "You're in the newspaper, and they're publishing your salary and talking about when you screw things up. It can be hard on kids. You need to talk it over." When ASML's Wennink was first asked to be CEO, he said no. "It was for private reasons," he shares. "My wife was not in a good place at the time, and I believe a strong home base is vital when taking on a job with so many responsibilities."

## Elevate Your Perspective While Boldly Delivering Results

In 2002, Harvard Kennedy School professors Ronald Heifetz and Marty Linsky introduced a new metaphor into management literature—the concept of "getting off the dance floor and going to the balcony." The metaphor juxtaposes delivering on daily work (being on the dance floor) with stepping back and seeing the big picture (being on the balcony). The most effective leaders, according to Heifetz and Linsky, are those with the ability to do both at once. This metaphor is particularly useful as your candidacy for the top job develops. During that time, it's vital that you keep the following actions in mind:

- Don't miss a step on the dance floor—deliver on your day job.
- Climb onto a higher balcony to hone your view of the future, the company, and the company's stakeholders.
- Be bold, whether on the balcony or the dance floor.

From the dance-floor perspective, don't forget that job number one is the job you're in. When Mary Barra stepped into the role of chief HR officer (CHRO) at General Motors, she chose not to focus on the next job. Instead, she embraced the CHRO position and proceeded to redefine talent management, leadership development, compensation, benefits, health care, organizational transformation, and other HR systems. "Do the job you're doing today like you're going to do it for the rest of your life," she advises, "because that means you're going to invest in it, you're going to make it better, and you're going to drive efficiencies."[3] HCA Healthcare's Sam Hazen reinforces the point: "The best way to move up is to continue to do your job really well," he says. "Produce results, do it in the right way, and continue to develop yourself. When opportunities present themselves, you'll be better prepared."

When it comes to being on the balcony, there are three perspectives you'll want to hone: that of the industry, the organization, and the stakeholder.

Having a strong point of view about your industry will help you both get and keep the job. As Stephen Schwarzman, CEO of Blackstone, shares, "Part of being successful when you're in the role is imagining what will happen before it happens." Elevance Health's Gail Boudreaux shares her experience: "I formed a perspective on the pillars that I felt were going to be really important. It helped me show up in good form.

It also meant that once I was chosen, the board was already familiar with my thinking, so that was helpful as well." Michael Wirth, CEO of Chevron, expands on the benefits of forming a point of view in advance of taking the job. "I took the time to deeply reflect on where I thought the world was going, where our industry was going, and where our company needed to change to stay relevant and competitive in that environment," he recollects. That time of reflection led him to adopt a simple litmus test for decision-making: Does this deliver financial performance while reducing carbon emissions? "It gave me a framework to engage with stakeholders," he shares. He says to them: "Here's how I'm thinking about the industry and the world, and here's how I think our company needs to respond to these things. What do you see differently?"

The next viewpoint involves looking more broadly across the whole organization—far beyond your area of responsibility. This is easier to do if, during your career, you've rotated across roles in various parts of the business. During the final ascent, however, switching jobs might not be a good idea. "I've seen too many candidates who, two years out, make the mistake of moving to roles where they don't have time to succeed," offers former Westpac CEO Gail Kelly. "It becomes a recipe for disaster." It's better to broaden your perspective during the final ascent by getting involved in enterprise-level projects, committees, and development programs; to learn about other parts of the organization; and to take an explicit company-first perspective in your decision-making (even if it's not the best answer for your specific area of responsibility).

The third view from the balcony is the stakeholder landscape. CEOs of today's large companies must have a point of view on a wide variety of societal and environmental issues. Accordingly, they must have a keen sense of employee, customer, and board sentiments and use them to help shape their company's principles as issues emerge. It takes real time and effort to form thoughtful, educated, institution-level (versus personal) points of view on issues such as responsible AI, rising inequality, political polarization, geopolitical instability, deteriorating climate, and so on.

A trip wire to be wary of, both on the balcony and the dance floor, is risk aversion. Savvy boards are well aware of the conclusive evidence that companies led by CEOs who lack the courage to make bold moves are unlikely to outperform the competition. Westpac's Kelly uses a cricket analogy to illustrate the point: "As a CEO candidate, you can't just defend the wicket and hope that you don't get out. You must step up and hit the ball . . . never, ever say to yourself, 'What I've done is enough.'" Adobe's Shantanu Narayen draws a contrast between "road builders" and more-suited-to-the-C-suite "flag planters." According to Narayen, road builders "don't care about *which* hill they need to climb; they just want to know what they need to do tomorrow." By contrast, the job of flag planters is to boldly look ahead and "figure out where to build the road." Narayen emphasizes that, as a CEO, "you should do more flag-planting," which is a skill you can hone on the way up.

Take Barra at General Motors. One of the first things she did on taking the HR role was to abolish the company's ten-page dress code and replace it with two words: "Dress appropriately."[4] Doing so was less about clothing than about signaling her willingness to take on General Motors' hundred-year-old, stodgy, paternal culture and shift it to one that recognized and empowered employees' own instincts. Such boldness helped her stand out from her peers in the eyes of the CEO and board as the right leader to take the company into the future.

## Round Out Your Profile with Humility

When asked, 88 percent of Americans will say they're above-average drivers.[5] In the ability to get along with others, 25 percent of students rate themselves in the top 1 percent.[6] When couples are asked to estimate their individual contributions to household work, the combined total routinely exceeds 100 percent.[7] These are all statistical impossibilities. They're also great examples of how we're predisposed to overrate our abilities and contributions. As an aspiring CEO candidate, it's important to have the humility to recognize your inherent, self-serving bias and counteract it through the following steps:

- Objectively assess your capabilities versus what's needed.
- Fill your skill gaps and gauge your progress on the way.
- Refuse to play politics in the process.

Assessing your capabilities starts with understanding what the company needs in its next leader. Brad Smith, the former CEO of financial software giant Intuit, uses a horse-racing analogy: "The reason there are very few Triple Crown winners," he says, "is because the Kentucky Derby is a very different track from the Preakness, which are both different from the Belmont. The right horse will win on the right track. If you're a candidate, first ask yourself in an intellectually honest way, 'What does the company most need?' and then 'Do I have that skill set today?'"

To understand if you have what's needed, where you stand, analyze your abilities along at least four dimensions. The first is breadth of experience and record (for example, leading transformational change, delivering a profit-and-loss statement, and representing the company externally). Second is knowledge and expertise (as it relates to such things as financial acumen, sales leadership, technology, target markets, and industry trends). Third is leadership skill (for example, your ability to think strategically, establish executive presence, build teams, and show self-awareness). Fourth is strength of your relationships and overall reputation. How are you viewed by internal stakeholders, such as your boss, peers, direct reports, and influencers? How about by external stakeholders, such as investors, customers, suppliers, regulators, and community leaders? And how do board members size you up? Michael Dell, founder and CEO of Dell Technologies, summarizes success on this dimension as whether you have followership. "The best definition of a leader," he reflects, "is if people are willing to follow you."

To help break through your self-serving bias, it's important to seek others' views. That might involve getting feedback from mentors, confidants, peers, and so on, but more often than not, you should ask someone else to gather that 360-degree information. The person who collects the feedback could be a trusted colleague, but most often, it's an external coach. While some leaders view having a coach as a weakness, the best point to the sporting world, where no player or team gets to the championship without a great coach. Nasdaq's Adena Friedman shares, "Before I became CEO, I was getting 360s and coaching over a period of years. The coach gathered all the feedback. Then I sat down with them, and we discussed it together. It helped crystalize the feedback into ideas for improvement and action." Robert Smith, founder and CEO of private equity firm Vista Equity Partners, explains the value of doing so. "If you're right-handed, you usually have a weak left hand." A great coach, he suggests, helps you see, "What's your left hand? What are you weak at that you can learn to be better at? And what are the things you need?"

Once you've assessed how you score along these four dimensions, it's time to start improving yourself. Think of it as embarking on a learning journey that involves cycles of taking action and then reflecting with a close group of advisors on the progress being made. Such journeys typically combine ongoing leadership coaching with participation in various forums or roundtables, visits to other companies, targeted reading lists, briefings from experts, and finding opportunities to gain experience and build relationships by dealing with the media, presenting to the board, and representing the company externally.

Pursuing this path requires striking a delicate balance. Without being seen as self-promoting or currying favor, you'll want to increase your visibility so those who need to know are aware that you want to make the final ascent. "I've seen this go awry so many times when people begin to run for the job," shares Intuit's Smith. "They almost campaign for the role, and that's the quickest way to throw you off track."

Westpac's Kelly shares her keys to success: "Don't play politics. Don't undermine people. None of that ends well. Be authentic, transparent, a team player, and an active supporter of colleagues for the greater good, even if they're also in the running for the role." Her advice reinforces the importance of taking a gut check of your motivations and intentions. If they're not sustainable, you simply won't be able to walk the line with authenticity. CCHMC's Fisher summarizes how it all comes together: "It's a quiet ambition pursued with humility. You gain confidence as you go by learning and growing every day."

Getting the balance right doesn't just stand you in good stead as a CEO candidate. It's also a win for the institution. What company isn't better off for having more service-oriented leaders connecting across the enterprise and boldly solving for the good of the whole organization—especially if they're doing so while delivering on their core responsibilities, building their self-awareness, and developing new capabilities and more fruitful relationships?

## Understand the CEO Selection Process and Put Your Best Foot Forward

There's a point in the climb from the final camp on Mount Everest to the summit where the mountaineer reaches what's called the "South Summit" and knows they're just a couple of hours from their dream coming true. But there is one obstacle in the way: a four-hundred-foot-long knife-edge ridge, where a single mistake could result in a two-mile drop down the side of the mountain. According to climbers, "You will gasp upon seeing it. It is steep and looks truly nasty."[8]

When you're formally tapped to be in the CEO selection process, you'll likely have a similar mix of excitement and dread. While every board's process is unique, a typical one will involve the following steps:

1. Choosing a top-tier headhunting firm to identify the best candidates

2. Defining what the business needs from its next CEO

3. Determining which stakeholders will play roles in the process and at which stages

4. Conducting an initial search for potential candidates both inside and outside the company—including qualified executives not proactively looking to move

5. Narrowing the list through in-depth due diligence (often including 360-degree references)

6. Holding initial screening interviews to narrow the list to the strongest prospects (the headhunter typically does these interviews)

7. Further narrowing the candidate pool by applying detailed psychometric, personality, and competency assessments that allow candidates to be easily scored and compared

8. Conducting the final stage of interviews to explore each candidate's vision for the company, leadership qualities, and how well they match the desired profile of the next CEO

9. Doing further due diligence on the preferred candidate, with their consent (including an identity check, a credit check, and a deeper background check to ensure no other disqualifications exist)

10. Making sure that all relevant stakeholders are confident in the preferred candidate's suitability and then formally making an offer

The good news is that if you've followed the advice we've already shared, you're already well prepared for many of the board's inquiries. You'll be able to articulate why you want the role. You'll have a bold vision for where the company should go next and how value will be created across the portfolio. You'll also have translated that into a perspective on what the company needs from its next CEO and be able to make a fact-based argument that your experience, knowledge, leadership skills, and relationships make you the right horse for the course. You'll be prepared to talk about how you've grown over the past three to five years yet also be clear-eyed and honest about your areas of weakness and how you'll need to surround yourself with others who can help in those areas. You'll also have built a following among your colleagues by leading authentically and helping others.

That said, the knife-edge ridge is no place to start winging it. "Probably the single most important responsibility the board has is CEO selection," CCHMC's Fisher explains. "They take it very seriously, and so should you. Prepare, prepare, prepare." Fisher, who has served as CEO of three different organizations, made it a point to rehearse his pitch and be mock-interviewed multiple times by his closest advisors, encouraging them to play the role of the cynic. Thanks to this preparation, he was able, during his actual interviews, to anticipate questions and have crisp and compelling answers. He also had a second set of eyes on any written material submitted into the process. Fisher's successes validate the famous assertion attributed to American football coach Vince Lombardi: "The will to win is not nearly as important as the will to prepare to win."

We've supported numerous executives as they made their way to the summit. Reflecting on this experience, our top ten less-obvious yet high-impact nuggets of advice for putting your best foot forward in the formal selection process are as follows, in no particular order:

- The headhunter is your ambassador to the search committee. Respect them and the process they've set up. (Don't try to work around it.)

- Every interaction is part of the interview process. Show your best self, whether it's in formal settings (such as presentations and interviews) or informal settings (such as dinners and ad hoc discussions).

- You'll be up against outsiders with fresh and bold perspectives. Make sure that you have an outsider's perspective while being clear on why being an insider is advantageous.

- Connect the dots for people—you know your story, but they don't. It's up to you to put it together for them in a way that makes sense and is easy to comprehend.

- Boards, not the sitting CEO, choose the new CEO. Don't mistake positive (or negative) signals from the incumbent for surefire signs of your standing in the process.

- Prepare not only for business-related interview topics but also for personal ones (for example, "Tell us about some formative experiences that have helped you build resilience").

- Listen closely to what's being asked and the subtext beneath it, and in responding, strive for brevity, clarity, and memorability.

- Don't just prepare the content. Think through how you want your audience to feel when you leave the room (and adjust your approach accordingly).

- Interviews are a two-way process. Ask questions that help you understand what your mandate will be, and make sure that the job will be one you want to have.

- As in other parts of the journey, authenticity matters. You may be able to fake it in an interview, but you're not going to be able to fake it as a CEO.

While we've directed most of our advice here toward internal CEO candidates, much of it also applies to those courting a CEO role outside their current organization. We've also tried to make the insights relevant regardless of the role one has during the final ascent, whether you're the COO, the CFO, or the head of a business unit. That said, we encourage leaders to also take into account nuances that are specific to the position they hold in the lead-up to the selection process.

For example, if you're a CFO shooting for the CEO job, you may have an extra burden to show that you see a picture bigger than just the numbers, that you're willing to take risks on new concepts with no precedent, and that you can motivate and engage colleagues through stories as well as facts. If you are a COO, you'll need to persuade the board that you can think strategically, are familiar with enterprise-wide issues, and have experience dealing with stakeholders. Divisional CEOs, for their part, will likely face additional scrutiny on peer relationships, their breadth of knowledge, and how well they understand resource allocation across business lines.

---

"We might succeed or not; that's not important," assert experienced Mount Everest alpinists.[9] "The summit is such a small piece of the mountain. Most of the beauty and wonders are experienced during the climb." The ascent to the CEO role is similar. The learning from the journey will be invaluable and, more than likely, help you summit other beautiful mountains, if that remains your aspiration. If you do set foot on the highest peak, we'll offer our congratulations—you're among the world's most elite business mountaineers.

So take a deep breath, and get ready for new heights.

> *It is when we are in transition that we are most completely alive.*
> —WILLIAM BRIDGES

CHAPTER TWO

# Starting Strong: Making Your CEO Transition a Catalyst for Renewal

Some experiences in life simply can't be prepared for. You can imagine how you might feel and what you might do, but you can never actually know how you will respond in a situation until it happens. Falling in love, becoming a parent, and facing one's mortality all fit into this category. In the workplace, your first interview, first day on the job, and the first time you're given the responsibility of managing others fall into this category. For a select few who successfully climb the corporate ladder, becoming CEO also lands there. Oliver Bäte, CEO of European financial services company Allianz, puts it starkly: "You don't really know what happens on the job until the day you have it."

What makes the top job so different from the leadership roles that come before it? To start with, new CEOs discover quickly that they're accountable for everything. Adobe's Shantanu Narayen explains how accountability shifts the moment you start the job: "The day you're announced CEO, your role changes drastically. Before, you had peers, and now they're looking at you to make the call." Second, the job is more isolating than most imagine. Gail Boudreaux, the CEO of Elevance Health, shares, "I don't think the loneliness of leading is overstated. As a division leader, CFO, or someone running a big part of the company, you're part of the team. Of course, you're still part of the team as CEO, but you're the coach, and the coach has a different relationship with the players than the players have with each other." Another unique aspect of the role is that after years of reporting to one boss, you'll now have ten or more in the form of the board—each of whom works part time.

For these reasons and many others, no one should assume that they have it all figured out when transitioning into the role of CEO. In fact, one-third to one-half of new CEOs are considered to be failing within eighteen months of taking the role, and more than 90 percent of those CEOs confess that they wish that they'd managed their transition differently. Those who get it right realize early on that they will need to lead differently than they did on the way to the top. They know that their success will depend on whether they can reinvent themselves by rewiring the many work habits they built up over decades (on average, new CEOs have worked for twenty-four years before taking the role). "CEOs peter out because they think they've arrived when they get the job instead of seeing it as a new beginning and a chance to regenerate themselves," observes HCA Healthcare's Sam Hazen.

Savvy CEOs recognize that the renewal opportunity isn't just for them but for the entire organization. A transition of leadership creates what German American psychologist Kurt Lewin refers to as an "unfreezing" moment for the institution. According to Lewin's theory, organizations exist in an equilibrium state largely constrained ("frozen") by resistance to change and group conformity. Movement becomes possible only when there is a jolt to the system (an "unfreezing"). Such jolts often come in the form of a crisis, whether company-specific (e.g., a safety or ethical conduct issue, hostile takeover attempt, or cyber breach) or external-event driven (e.g., a pandemic, natural disaster, or international conflict). A CEO transition creates a similar opportunity—without the crisis—to reset an organization's aspirations and ways of working.

The best CEOs don't miss the opportunity to make their first six to twelve months (not just the vaunted hundred days) both a personal transition of great import and a profound moment of institutional renewal. As PepsiCo's Ramon Laguarta puts it, "Everybody's ready for change. Everybody's expecting change. They would be disappointed if you didn't." While each leader will act in ways befitting their unique situation, there are at least four common ingredients for success:

- Not making it about you
- Listening, then acting
- Nailing your firsts
- Playing "big ball"

## Don't Make It About You

In his 1980 book *Transitions: Making Sense of Life's Changes*, consultant William Bridges wrote about the difference between transition and change. According to Bridges, change is something that happens to people. Transition, on the other hand, is internal: It's what happens in people's minds as they go through change. Change can happen very quickly, while transition usually occurs more slowly. The distinction is subtle but vital to understand for a new CEO who is pursuing both personal and institutional renewal.

The day you become CEO, all the attention becomes laser-focused on you, often in ways that distort reality. Says Allianz's Bäte, "People change their face when you become CEO. Everybody gives you partial information. All of a sudden, you have a lot more friends. You have much funnier jokes. Your ties are much more beautiful than they were the day before." This magnifies the sense of your own power. Nasdaq's Adena Friedman adds, "Once you become CEO, the relationship with the team changes, and what used to be a suggestion or idea is suddenly taken as a 'command,' which was certainly not the intention."

Etsy's Josh Silverman shares an example of the power of the CEO chair from his time leading his former company, the invitation website Evite. "One day, rumors went rampant across Evite that we were selling the company. I asked my executive assistant why everyone suddenly thought that, and she said it was because I had changed the position of my desk. It used to be that everyone could see my screen when they walked out the door, and then I changed it 180 degrees so no one could see my screen. They assumed I had something to hide, and if I had something to hide, it must mean we're selling the company."[1]

All this attention and power can quickly create a celebrity CEO phenomenon where the transition becomes all about you. Dr. Robert Grossman, CEO of the hospital system NYU Langone Health, observes, "I see a lot of CEOs who are very much about themselves. They have a lot of ego, and some arrogance . . . and they view the job as a destination, not a journey." By contrast, successful CEOs don't let power go to their heads—they keep their minds focused on the institution. "I think when you're a CEO, you're the concierge," Dr. Grossman continues, "and you're responsible for the care and feeding of your institution."

Former CEO of Merck Ken Frazier shares his leadership approach:

"I thought it was important to be humble. My dad was a janitor, and he was ten feet tall in my eyes. I understood that when people came into my office, they were speaking to the CEO—they weren't speaking to Ken Frazier. I also knew that when I was in that chair, my job was to serve my employees and patients; it wasn't about me. People respect the chair, and when you are in that position, you need to do what you can to leave the place in better shape than you found it."

This advice to think beyond oneself sounds laudable in theory, but what does it mean in practice? It all starts with asking different questions, which then lead to different answers, as shown in the table below.

### Are You Asking the Right Questions?

| | ⊘ "It's about me" questions | ✓ "It's not about me" questions |
|---|---|---|
| **Vision** | What legacy will I leave? | What organizational purpose do I serve? |
| **Leadership** | What are my "nonnegotiable" expectations of others? | Who does the company need me to be? |
| **Team** | Who on my team will complement my weaknesses? | What conditions will I need to put in place to maximize my team's success? |
| **Change** | What is broken that needs fixing? | How will we respect our past while accelerating or disrupting our future? |
| **Engagement** | How will I get the organization on board with my vision? | How will I engage the organization in creating our shared vision? |
| **Measurement** | How will I know if I'm successful? | How will we know if we're winning? |

Etsy's Silverman has embodied the "it's not about me" mindset. "When you're building a business, you're going to go through hard times," he says. "You and your team all have to have a shared belief in something bigger than yourselves, the stock price, or the market cap. Finding that key purpose is important, and then you can frame everything in terms of service to that purpose."[2] As for his personal ambition, Silverman tells us, "I don't want to spend a lot of time on any endeavor that I don't think will have a purpose greater than myself. It's not about having the job. It's about aspiring to do something really meaningful and seeing the job as a means to that end."

## Listen, Then Act

When a new CEO takes over, anxiety levels can run high within the organization. Everyone wants to hear what the new person thinks, what will change, and what that change will mean for them. With people over-analyzing every word and move the new CEO says and makes, the urge to decide, declare, promise, and explain is strong. The best leaders in transition know that it's better to listen and find out what's really going on before making broad declarations or premature moves. Of course, context matters—in a turnaround situation, there'll be a premium on action—but in most contexts successful leaders adopt Albert Einstein's approach: "If I had an hour to solve a problem and my life depended on the solution, I would spend the first fifty-five minutes understanding the problem." Practically speaking, this way forward translates to the following practices:

- Start with a broad-based listening tour.
- Create a fact-based "one version of the truth."
- Lock in a short list of bold moves.
- Communicate those moves in an elegantly simple, engaging manner.

Like virtually all successful CEOs, Elevance Health's Boudreaux began her tenure with a listening tour. "I really did spend the first year traveling all over the company," she says. "We re-identified the mission, vision, and values of the company . . . and then we tested it with employees in one-on-ones, lunch meetings, and so on, using that time to refine our thinking." A successful listening tour should include all key stakeholders and involve hard-hitting questions. "The first thing I did was go out and talk to clients," shares Nasdaq's Friedman. "What's working? What's not working? What can we do better? Where do you see us as a strategic partner? Where do you not see us as a strategic partner? Where would you want us to be focused?" Lockheed Martin's former CEO Marillyn Hewson explains why such questions are uniquely powerful during the transition period: "People tell you things when you're the newbie that they're not going to tell you in two or three years."

The perceptions you pick up during your listening tour should be validated by facts where possible and augmented by analytics—which will help you answer tough questions about the state of the business. The goal is to create one version of the truth that you can use as a baseline for the organization's aspirations and against which you can judge its future performance. Financial and operational metrics are key, but so are metrics on talent, teamwork, culture, and stakeholder perceptions. JPMC's Jamie Dimon says, "Early on, there needs to be a lot of probing, a lot of asking questions, and a lot of reading what people give you." He warns, "People manipulate the numbers and make things look good. . . . You've got to say, 'What are the real facts? What are the details?'"

Once you have a strong, fact-based understanding about what is needed to propel the business forward, it's time to identify those actions that will really move the needle. What will you buy and sell? Where will you invest? How will you improve productivity? Where will you create more differentiation? How will you reallocate capital? McKinsey research shows that making even two big moves across these arenas more than doubles the likelihood of rising from mid- to top-tier performance, while executing three or more makes such a rise six times more likely.[3] Further, CEOs who make these moves earlier in their tenure outperform those who move later, so there's a premium on mobilizing the organization quickly. As Adobe's Narayen puts it, "You need to decide, what are the one or two things that I can do that will move the needle at the organizational level? There are fifty things that are table stakes that won't inspire anyone. If I can talk about one or two things that can get a twinkle in your eye, I've done my job."

You may be wondering, "If moving fast is important, why do great CEOs invest so much time in listening first?" Nasdaq's Friedman shares her rationale: "We shaped our strategy discussions in the first year as a team because I wanted it to be the team's creation. I wanted them to own it from the start." S&P Global's Doug Peterson reinforces the point: "It's important for people to feel like they're part of developing the strategy of the company, that they belong, and that they're included." Friedman's and Peterson's experiences are supported by social science that suggests people are up to five times more motivated to execute initiatives that they've had a hand in creating versus ones that have been handed down from on high. Investing time to gain involvement and build ownership has a strong return on investment.

A powerful tool to mobilize the organization is to distill the company's transformational vision and strategy down to an elegantly simple "one-pager," or even a handful of well-chosen words. For example, early in his tenure, former Morgan Stanley CEO James Gorman invited a business professor to speak about strategy to a large group of his senior executives. He heard a lot of interesting ideas, but none that truly captured the essence of what the company was trying to do. He seized the moment and stepped up to the podium. "In seventy-two words, I laid out the strategy," Gorman says. "There were some deep, coded messages in those seventy-two words, which are still sitting on a piece of paper on my desk. Clarity of message is key." At Singaporean multinational banking and financial services corporation DBS Bank, CEO Piyush Gupta leveraged visual elements as well: "We put together a one-page visual we call the DBS House. Everything's on it: our vision, strategy, values, targets, et cetera. It allows us to all speak the same language about what we want to do and, more importantly, what we don't want to do."

## Nail Your Firsts

In a famous social science experiment conducted in 1946 by psychologist Solomon Asch, participants were given one of two sentences. The first read, "Steve is smart, diligent, critical, impulsive, and jealous." The second read, "Steve is jealous, impulsive, critical, diligent, and smart." Although both sentences contained the same information, the first one led with positive traits while the second one started with negatives. When asked to evaluate what they thought of Steve, subjects who were given the first sentence evaluated him more positively than those given the second. This is an example of what social scientists refer to as the "primacy effect," and it's why the adage "You never get a second chance to make a first impression" matters—first impressions tend to last.

Early in your tenure, everyone, even those you have worked with for years, is forming their first impression of you *as the CEO*. Getting your first impressions right will send strong messages about how you intend to lead differently (from the previous CEO, as well as versus how you've led in previous roles) and that you're serious about renewing the organization. Applying the following four principles will go a long way to ensuring that your first impressions are positive:

- Understand people's "why?"
- Keep to a single narrative.
- Err on the side of complete candor.
- Prepare intensely for moments of truth.

If you know what motivates a person and can connect at that level, the chances are greater that you'll make a positive and lasting impression. "What drives different people varies widely," says Allianz CEO Bäte. To understand people, he explains, "you need to go beyond just listening to what they say and think about what they really mean." Lockheed Martin's Hewson expands further: "If you take time to understand why they're saying what they're saying, you can then help shape their longer-term thinking." Netflix CEO Reed Hastings gives an example of how understanding the "why?" of the press shapes his actions: "They want to be truth tellers, but they're forced to be entertainers." Hastings makes it a point to give reporters a bit of both truth and entertainment and can convey his message more effectively as a result.

ASML's Peter Wennink hews to the second positive-impression principle: sticking to a single narrative. He shares, "What we told the supervisory board, I told the investors. It was exactly the same transparency I use within my team." Taking this approach is liberating—as one CEO confided, "I'm not smart enough to have two versions of the truth!" On the other hand, you'll need to brace yourself to endure, in the words of Procter & Gamble's former CEO A. G. Lafley, "excruciating repetition." Once you know the story inside out, it's easy to assume incorrectly that other people will take it in quickly and see all the implications that you see. The best CEOs recognize that when people hear a story for the first time, they're so busy processing what they hear and trying to work out what it means that they can't possibly appreciate all the nuances.

Former Israel Discount Bank CEO Lilach Asher-Topilsky speaks about the third principle in nailing your firsts—candor: "Don't overpromise. Be frank about the problems, not just the opportunities." Even if you're uncomfortable in the moment, such sincerity lays the foundation for real trust and credibility. To facilitate this level of candor with their boards, virtually every excellent CEO we've spoken to starts board meetings with an executive session (just the CEO and the board). During this time, they share a list of things that are going well, matched by an equal number that aren't. Doing so offers directors a better perspective on what the CEO is dealing with, which allows them a chance to give better guidance. Elevance Health's Boudreaux clarifies at what level to have the discussion: "It's not that you're going to tell board members every operating detail—that's not their job—but you need to tell them the things that matter. You don't ever want to surprise your board."

U.S. Bancorp's former CEO Richard Davis shares how candor translates to communicating with investors: "I often told them, 'Look, you deserve the truth, and we deserve for you to believe us. So when we tell you that things are going amazingly well, you will remember us telling you when they weren't.'" IBM's Arvind Krishna encourages leaders to schedule hard conversations with stakeholders sooner rather than later. "If you defer something hard, it actually becomes harder, taking more time and effort," he says. "When you open up a conversation, the hard part's behind you, and you can actually move on with less effort."

Successful CEOs prepare intensely for important moments of truth, such as the first time they have their team together, their first board meeting, their first investor presentation, and their first quarterly earnings report. Greg Case, CEO of the global professional services firm Aon, learned this the hard way. When he took the top job at the company, he was told he had to present at an investor day that was scheduled to take place a month after he arrived. Having come in from the outside, he knew there wasn't time to prepare a thoughtful, compelling, and meaningful view of the firm's future strategy. Case recalls, "Had I been more seasoned, I would have said: 'We're going to cancel that.' But I didn't know any better. So I said, 'Okay, we'll get ready.' It was a massive fire drill from hell."

Moments of truth also include early interactions with individual board members. Nasdaq's Friedman shares her hard-won learning: "The one thing I didn't do enough of when I first started was scheduling individual meetings with the board members. I thought, 'Okay, I'm done with this board meeting—on to the next board meeting.' But then board members began reaching out saying, 'Adena, I'd like to be able to give you my individual feedback.'" Friedman eventually formalized that feedback-gathering process, meeting with individual board members twice a year to establish one-on-one connections. Those candid conversations enabled both sides to share concerns and, over time, forged trust.

Note that building an open, trust-based relationship with the chairperson is particularly important, so much so that NYU Langone Health's Dr. Grossman advises, "If you don't think you can build a good relationship with your chair, you shouldn't take the role. And over time, that relationship has to grow, and it has to be mutually respectful." Westpac's Gail Kelly describes the cadence she established with her chairman: "I was very respectful of his time. We got into a pattern where every Friday, regardless of where he or I was, I'd ring him. I had my agenda of issues we needed to tackle. We also had regular conversations such as, 'I'm just a little worried about X; I'm not sure it's going to go well.'"

Getting your first impressions right doesn't guarantee success, but it does increase the odds. As in golf, putting the first shot far down the fairway is the way you want to play.

## Play "Big Ball"

"Play big ball, not small ball," advises Sandy Cutler, the former CEO of power management company Eaton. "By that, I mean spend time on things that no one else can in ways that magnify your effectiveness without getting mired in things that don't make a difference."

This advice may sound like common sense, but it's too often not common practice for new CEOs who suddenly find themselves accountable for everything and to everyone. Many new CEOs enter the role thinking that they'll go hard for the first ninety days and then back off a bit. That's easier said than done. "I didn't know whether I'd be successful, and so I went 100 percent, totally all in," divulges former LEGO CEO Jørgen Vig Knudstorp. "My health suffered quite badly. I went to a checkup, and the doctor said, 'You have the fitness of a sixty-five-year-old.' I was, at the time, just approaching forty. I then started becoming a bit more sensible." Etsy's Silverman learned a similar lesson. "I thought if I was in meetings all day every day, seven days a week, ten hours a day, that was being hyperproductive," he says. "But much of that was really counterproductive, not just to me but to my team as well. I'm better now at directing my energy than I was before."[4]

Knudstorp's and Silverman's experiences are cautionary tales—as a new CEO, you should be disciplined about playing "big ball" from day one. To play big ball throughout your tenure, you can put three foundational elements in place early:

- **Time management:** Set clear boundaries and stay extremely disciplined.

- **Talent:** Put A players in critical roles, move C players out, and help B players succeed.

- **Operating rhythm:** Combine accountability with urgency and targeted coaching.

S&P Global's Peterson shares how he approached time management: "Time is a precious resource for a CEO. If somebody asked me, 'What do you do every day?' I'd say, 'Well, every day is different.' But if they asked, 'What do you do every quarter?' that's where I'd be able to think about how I divided my time between different constituencies over a much longer period. Once I had that perspective, it was easier for me to say, 'Let's send our CFO to a meeting,' or 'Maybe we should incorporate this meeting into a larger event where stakeholders are already present, such as the World Economic Forum.'" Like Peterson, virtually all of the excellent CEOs we spoke to put boundaries on the amount of time they spend on various categories of activity. Their administrative assistant or chief of staff manages their calendar accordingly such that something new is added only if another is taken off.

Dr. Flemming Ørnskov, CEO of the Swiss dermatology leader Galderma, shares the hardest part of getting balance: "The thing I had to learn was to say no. When someone calls me and says, 'I want you to be the keynote speaker' or 'Don't you want to do this off-site?' or 'Let's do a dinner,' saying no feels uncomfortable initially, because people mean it in a friendly way. But to say no politely is important." For Dr. Ørnskov, saying "no" to such things equates to saying "yes" to being as disciplined and productive as possible in what *is* taken on. "I really prepare for meetings and make sure the agenda is tight and focused," he explains. "I read the material, I think about it, I start and finish meetings on time. All meetings start and end with a recap of action items and follow-ups."

S&P Global's Peterson shares a tip he learned on how to know when to say no: "I actually have a little test my admin and I use," he says. "Whenever an invitation comes in for something that's weeks or months out, we think forward and ask ourselves, 'If this was being asked for today or tomorrow, would I be asking why I'm doing this?' If that's true, then we say 'no' right now and we just don't do it."

The second area to get right early is talent management. GE CEO Larry Culp summarizes why: "Your people decisions are really where all your leverage is. As a CEO, you absolutely have to get those right." Adobe's Narayen expands, "Build your company on the superpowers of people who are the best at what they do and who are working in the areas that are most important and impactful for the company." In practice, this translates into creating a short list of roles (thirty to fifty) that will have the most impact on driving the company's strategy and then making sure those roles are filled with A players whose superpowers fit the role.

The best CEOs also make tough calls on C players, even those who've been loyal to the organization for decades. Doing so isn't easy.

Says Adobe's Narayen: "The hardest decisions are about how to have conversations with people when the company has outgrown them." Although those encounters may be difficult, JPMC's Dimon reinforces the importance of having them: "If we were 'loyal' to them by leaving them in the job, we'd be hugely disloyal to everyone else and to the company's clients."

Often neglected on a CEO's talent management priority list is creating the conditions for B players to up their game. This means you should be acting as a role model, setting expectations, and providing incentives and capability-building opportunities. Having done so, if no improvement happens in a discrete time frame (months, not years), it's time for a colleague to move on. Westpac's Kelly explains why: "It very rarely gets better if you've put the conditions in place for their success and they aren't succeeding. That's why you want to make those decisions early. It's the most elegant way of dealing with it, because you can discuss what's not the right fit. If you let it go on too long, you can't have that discussion."

The third foundational element that will enable you as CEO to play big ball is establishing a robust operating rhythm for the company. As Merck's Frazier says, "You have to figure out how to work together, making sure the company has the right intensity, operational cadence, and accountability. It's great to have a mission, but you have to deliver what you say you will deliver." This is harder than it may seem because it also means deciding the altitude at which you will fly and how involved you'll be. As the corporate CEO, you have business unit CEOs reporting to you who have the operating responsibility you no longer have. Although you will need to empower those people, there is a trap to avoid, as GE's Culp explains: "I've seen a lot of my peers giving their business unit CEOs a lot of room because that's what they always wanted when they were in the role. Then someone surprises them in a not-good way, and they start to think differently."

The best CEOs take the time early in their tenure to think through the tempo and template for accountability and execution. This means playing a hands-on role in setting up weekly, monthly, quarterly, and annual meetings with individuals, committees, the team as a whole, and the top hundred or so leaders. Although every company's operating rhythm is unique, a common template is to get the top team together weekly for a relatively informal sixty-minute meeting to touch base, monthly for a more formal half day, and once a year at an off-site. At minimum, one-on-ones between the CEO and their direct reports should take place monthly, and formal business reviews should be scheduled quarterly. The CEO and senior team also typically host a broader group of often hundreds of executives for a two- or three-day senior leadership conference at least once a year.

Whatever operating rhythm is chosen, it should continually be refined to ensure that it's serving its purpose. Former Best Buy CEO Hubert Joly points out, "The key with any stakeholder is to get the 'say–do' ratio right—the ratio between what we said we were going to do and what we actually did. That's how you get credibility. If you do what you say you'll do, they'll want to see less of you. They'll want you to spend your time working on the business and delivering on your commitments."

---

We began this chapter by discussing how, like falling in love, transitioning into the CEO role is something you can't fully prepare for. As such, it's a profoundly uncomfortable but also wondrous time for those fortunate enough to have been chosen to lead at the highest levels.

We also noted that the impact of the transition extends far beyond the leader. The ascension of a new CEO is an unfreezing moment that can catalyze significant institutional renewal.

GE's Culp describes how it feels when it all comes together: "I liken it to the flow I remember when I was on my high school basketball team. We ran fast, we took care of each other, and we were successful. Running fast with incredible people working at this level—I just find it to be great fun and rewarding in a whole host of ways."

By not making it about you, listening then acting, nailing your firsts, and playing big ball—you'll soon hit your stride.

> *Success breeds complacency.*
> *Complacency breeds failure.*
> —ANDY GROVE

CHAPTER THREE
# Staying Ahead: How the Best CEOs Continually Improve Performance

Most people know the fable "The Tortoise and the Hare." In the story, the two animals challenge one another to a race to prove who is faster. The hare starts strong and is soon out of sight. Mid-race, the hare lies down to rest, feeling certain that it's going to win. After a time, the tortoise plods past the place where the hare is sleeping peacefully. By the time the hare wakes up, it's too late to overtake the tortoise, despite its best efforts.

The tale originated with the Greek storyteller Aesop, who makes use of humble incidents to teach great truths. Today's CEOs are hardly in a simple race, however. Their reality is more akin to being chased by world-class drivers in state-of-the-art Formula 1 cars on a track full of unexpected turns, multiple surfaces, and unpredictable weather. Could the moral of the ancient slow and steady tortoise story still be relevant to the leaders of present-day megacorporations?

The answer is a clear "yes" if you're a CEO who started strong and is now riding high three to five years into your tenure. You did all the right things early in your role: Set a bold vision, pursued a short list of big strategic moves, put the right talent and accountability mechanisms in place, gained the trust of your stakeholders, and focused your time on what mattered. As a result, you have created significant value on your watch. Your fellow CEOs at other companies who didn't start as strong are, at worst, being ousted from the role and, at best, struggling with persistent performance challenges and increasingly skeptical stakeholders.

On one hand, this is exactly where you hoped you would be—congratulations! On the other hand, as Aesop's fable warns, you're about to face your toughest challenge yet: complacency. Said another way, becoming a successful CEO is hard, but staying successful is even harder. Research confirms this challenge: More than half of the companies on the Fortune 500 list in the year 2000 went bankrupt, were acquired, or ceased to exist in the following fifteen years.[1]

It's during this middle stretch of your CEO tenure that the concentration and energy you applied to your objectives during your first years on the job are most likely to dissipate and fragment. Intellectually, the danger of such complacency is simple to grasp. No one wants to be the prizefighter who wins the title belt, goes soft, and unceremoniously loses it to a hungrier up-and-comer—or to be the band whose single goes platinum, only to become known as a one-hit wonder down the road. We've never met a CEO who told us, "Yep, I'm becoming complacent." But we've met plenty who suddenly recognize that complacency has set in when they see a proverbial tortoise ahead of them.

Take one of the most respected, influential, and successful CEOs of the twenty-first century: Jamie Dimon at JPMC. During his early tenure, he deftly navigated the financial services behemoth through the global financial crisis of 2008; a year later, he was named in audit firm Brendan Wood International's list of TopGun CEOs.[2] Fast-forward to 2012, however, and Dimon was facing a crisis after his company got hit with a trading loss of approximately $6 billion. When asked what went wrong, Dimon confessed, "The big lesson I learned? Don't get complacent, despite a successful track record."[3]

The reasons why complacency sets in can be more emotional than intellectual. In the middle years of your CEO journey, you're the author of the organization's status quo. It's your plan. This makes it far more difficult for you to judge the business dispassionately and to disrupt what's working well enough. Also, with more success comes increased confidence in your judgment. "The problem with being a CEO a long time," says former Morgan Stanley boss James Gorman, "is everybody tells you that you have all the answers. It's comforting to your ego but very dangerous."[4] PepsiCo's Ramon Laguarta similarly warns, "The longer you're in this role, the greater the risk you think you know everything. You think you're a hero. You think you know it all. And you think you are the most intelligent person in the room. And you're not."

Like everything about the CEO role, the dynamics at play are as much about the institution as they are about you. When traditional competition is fading in the rearview mirror and emerging competitors are gathering their forces, it becomes increasingly difficult to define what winning looks like. Meanwhile, the license you had early on to shake things up has long expired, and your employees have become comfortable working in the new ways you introduced. Unless you're again the prime mover of change, the organization will begin to stagnate.

So how do CEOs avoid complacency and sustain high performance through the role's middle years? We don't pretend to have a magic formula, but from our continued research and experience in the field of CEO excellence, we're confident the odds are greatly increased by:

- Enhancing your learning
- Taking an outsider's perspective
- Collaboratively defining the next S-curve
- Future-proofing the organization

## Enhance Your Learning

In the early years of being a CEO, you learned an extraordinary amount. The conversations you had with customers, employees, investors, analysts, board members, and other stakeholders helped you shape the strategy that's led to the success you're enjoying today. Now you're flooded with requests to tell your story and share your wisdom with others. While these requests are well earned, Galderma's Dr. Flemming Ørnskov describes the dangers that lurk beneath. "There are so many distractions," he says. "You can win prizes; you can get accolades. Which [are] all good. But the main job you have is to do better every year than you did the year before."

The point isn't to pull back from external engagement. It's to make sure that you're spending time listening, learning, and connecting dots versus talking about your successes. In Dr. Ørnskov's case, his success early on allowed him to delegate more responsibility to his team, which meant he could actually spend *more* time outside the company—but only on things that would help the business stay competitive. "I knew all the key opinion leaders," he shares. "I spent an enormous amount of time on understanding what was going on, seeing patients, meeting doctors, going to scientific conferences to get the latest in research, and studying our competitors' moves." The time Dr. Ørnskov spent learning paid off: "The inspiration for at least two or three deals we did came from doctors I got to know who said to me, 'You should really think about this thing,' 'I'm involved in this product development,' or 'I've seen patients in this clinical trial.'"

Similarly, Aon's Greg Case uses client conversations to pick up new ideas including, for example, ones for cybersecurity and intellectual property theft products. Case explains his philosophy: "You, of course, interact with clients to serve them, but you also interact with them to understand how you want to change." For LEGO's Jørgen Vig Knudstorp, an unlikely group of customers was instrumental: the adult fan community. "They were viewed as a gray market and a little bit of a fringe group," he shares. He joined them for one of their conferences and gained their trust, and they helped him see what was possible. LEGO's adult customers now total more than one million people and account for 30 percent of LEGO's global business.

Many CEOs reach out directly to counterparts in other industries to learn from them. Etsy's Josh Silverman explains his ethos: "Unless I'm reaching out to people outside of our four walls and learning what true state of the art looks like, I'm missing a lot," he says. "I recommend seeking out who's best of breed and then starting to benchmark them." This can take the form of everything from quick virtual connections to making in-person field trips. Intuit's Brad Smith, for example, made it a point to shadow leaders in other companies once a quarter—sometimes bringing other Intuit executives along to learn as well. "I told the companies I visited that I just wanted to be a fly on the wall; this isn't a trade show," he says. He'd take notes throughout the day, share his observations at the end of it, and then write up a report on what he learned to share with his colleagues at Intuit. "They called it 'Uncle Brad's book report: Here's what I learned,'" shares Smith.

Councils of CEOs from multiple industries are often a valuable and efficient way to get perspectives from peers. Says Chevron CEO Michael Wirth, "The nice thing about a CEO council is that it's a very safe place. You have a chance to learn from one another and to help one another with the lessons that only CEOs really understand. It's hard to find somebody else to talk to about a lot of these things." Elevance Health's Gail Boudreaux shares the sentiment. "I've really valued, for example, chairing The Business Council and getting to know other CEOs," she shares. "In smaller forums, you can really talk about issues that you're worried about but that you're not going to share with everybody on your team."

Investors can be another important source of new ideas. General Mills' Ken Powell recalls, "I spent a lot of time with our top shareholders. There were, of course, some who wanted a quick hit, but there were others who were very constructive and had a long history of really understanding the industry. I got a lot of energy from those conversations, and they helped me refine or reinforce our thinking." Tuning in closely to activist investors can also be beneficial. S&P Global's Doug Peterson reveals, "I've always felt that we needed to stay informed on what activists were looking for, and so every year at our board, we bring in investment bankers to tell us what they're saying." Doing so helps him and his team, he says, "to be clear-headed about what fits and what doesn't fit, and how we are using our capital."

Beyond the investment community, the best CEOs generally don't shy away from engaging with and learning from their critics. IBM's Arvind Krishna listens to criticism of his company in the press. "The fact that our critics have a point of view means that they care and want us to do better," says Krishna. "If they're willing to spend time with me, I can learn from them."

Drawing on practices from other industries can also be powerful. For example, former Nestlé CEO Peter Brabeck-Letmathe had a revelation when he learned how Disney, as it began to conceive each animated film, was already thinking about how to make the most of that film over the next ten years. "So instead of creating just one ingredient for one product, which has limited value," shares Brabeck-Letmathe, "I was thinking about how to transform a nutritional ingredient into a brand and how to exploit it over the next ten years . . . People make things and do things in different ways, and you always can learn something and apply it in your own organization." Such learning can also be gleaned from advisors and bringing in talent from the outside. HCA Healthcare's Sam Hazen explains, "Consultants brought us very helpful outside perspectives on what other companies had done with their supply chains, HR, capital allocation, and so on." Hazen also hired some people from other companies in senior positions whom he frequently asked, "How'd y'all do this in your company?"

Learning doesn't just come from the outside. As Intuit's Smith shares, "I had two meetings a week with people many levels down in the organization and with eight to ten people in each group. To all, I posed three questions: 'What's getting better than it was six months ago? What's not making enough progress or going in the wrong direction? And what's something you're afraid no one is telling me that you believe I need to know?' It was incredible, because you skip levels and go right to the front lines of the area you're trying to learn about. You cut everybody else out and eliminate the filter."

Like Smith, JPMC's Dimon regularly gathers input from company employees by traveling to different branches and arranging in-person meetings. He also moved his CEO office from the corner of the building to the middle, right next to the elevators, so he could more easily exchange ideas and information with his team. ASML's Peter Wennink utilized an additional approach to achieve the same ends: "I had this habit of every morning going down into the cafeteria," he explains. "We have more than 20,000 people in Veldhoven [ASML's corporate headquarters], and everybody knew, 'He's there at 7:30, he's drinking his coffee and eating his croissant, and if you have a question, he's sitting there, you can ask him.' It gave me huge insights about things that were so obviously stupid that we did. The more distance you get between people on the floor and yourself as the company grows, the more things get filtered."

Finally, many CEOs also turn their learning journey inward to improve their self-awareness, foster creativity, and see possibilities that others may not. Salesforce CEO Marc Benioff describes how he tries to maintain an open mind when approaching challenges: "Shoshin [a concept from Zen Buddhism] is the beginner's mind. As a CEO, you've got a lot coming at you all the time. In your beginner's mind, you have every possibility, but in your expert's mind you have few," Benioff says.[5] "Every day, I have a meditation practice. . . . I need to have a beginner's mind, because what's happening today is very different from anything that's ever happened before." Medtronic's Bill George, who also practices meditation regularly, says, "The important thing is to have a set time each day to pull back from the intense pressures of leadership to reflect on what's happening. In addition to meditation, I know leaders who take time for daily journaling, prayer, and reflecting while walking, hiking, or jogging."

## Take an Outsider's Perspective

In one of Nobel Prize–winning psychologist Daniel Kahneman's experiments, a grocery store put Campbell's Soup products on sale for 79 cents with a sign above the display that read "limit twelve per customer."[6] Another grocery store ran the same sale but with no purchase limit. On average, how many cans were purchased per customer in the first store? Seven. And in the other store? Roughly three.

What's going on here, and why is this relevant? The experiment shows the power of what is called an "anchoring heuristic." A heuristic is essentially a mental shortcut or rule of thumb the brain uses to simplify complex decisions (also known as a cognitive bias). An anchor is a piece of information that someone relies on to make a decision. In the supermarket experiment, shoppers' brains anchored on the purchase limit of twelve and adjusted downward. Those who bought only three cans of soup didn't have the number twelve in mind, so they made what might be considered a more normal-size purchase, or one adjusting upward from zero.

Now let's apply this learning to the way many CEOs traditionally approach their strategy. Each year, these CEOs refresh their goals based on the prior year's assumptions—what still holds, and what doesn't? By contrast, the best CEOs periodically do thorough analyses of all aspects of their businesses in the same way that they did when they took the role, as though they were coming in from the outside with fresh eyes. They're not wed to the past, encumbered by internal loyalties, or willing to bow to short-term pressures.

Can an incumbent really act as boldly as an outsider? Yes. In the early 1980s when Intel's profits plummeted from $198 million one year to $2 million the next, then-president Andy Grove asked Gordon Moore, Intel's CEO at the time, what Moore thought would happen "if we got kicked out and the board brought in a new CEO."[7] Moore responded that a new CEO would get the company out of memory chips. Grove stared at him and asked, "Why shouldn't you and I walk out the door, come back, and do it ourselves?" The rest is history: Intel moved away from dynamic random-access memory chips and staked its future on a new product, the microprocessor. The move helped usher in a run of success for the company that lasted for decades.

Michael Dell of Dell Technologies found a novel way thirty years into his tenure to prompt his leadership team to think like outsiders. "I told them that we were going to have a new competitor five years from now. This company was going to be in every business that we're in, and they were going to be faster, more innovative, and lower cost than us. They were going to put us out of business." He followed up this grim prediction by saying, "The way we're going to prevent this, is we're going to become that company. Because if we don't do it, it'll be done *to* us." This thought experiment spurred hours of conversation among his leadership team as they rethought the company's future from the outside in.

While there are many methods CEOs can use to take an outsider's view, virtually all are grounded in asking for factual answers to a holistic set of questions:

## CAPITAL MARKETS

- What has driven our historic shareholder returns over various time horizons?
- How does our valuation stack up to that of our peers today, and why?
- What are the highest-impact levers to change our valuation (growth, margin improvement rates, et cetera)?

## STRATEGY

- Are we in the right businesses, geographies, sectors, product lines, and customer segments?
- How can we strengthen our competitive advantage in these chosen areas?
- What are our highest-potential merger, acquisition, partnership, and divestment opportunities?

## COMMERCIAL

- What are our opportunities for revenue growth (volume and pricing)?
- What is the current profitability of each area we choose to play in, and what is the potential?
- What are customers saying and competitors doing by channel, segment, and product?

## COST AND CAPITAL

- Where do we have direct and indirect cost improvement opportunities?
- How can we substantially enhance the return on investment (ROI) of our capital expenditures?
- How can we make our capital structure more resilient?

## ORGANIZATION

- What radical improvements can be made to communication and engagement?
- How can we improve our execution and speed (for example, through structure, incentives, and review cadence)?
- Where do we need to refresh talent and our talent proposition, and where do we need to build new capability?

## REPUTATION

- What is our impact on the environment, and how can it be improved?
- How do we perform on social topics (for example, diversity, well-being, and community involvement)?
- How strong is our governance model?

Those in the private equity world will recognize that this exercise takes a page right out of their playbook. In that world, an asset is reassessed every two or three years, and bold actions are taken accordingly. The idea is to view a company through the eyes of theoretical new owners looking to form a new investment thesis and, in doing so, acknowledge that both the company and the external environment will have changed meaningfully since the previous investment thesis was formed. It also encourages important voices of dissent to "speak truth to power" where needed. This thought process is helpful in any organization. "You have to reinvent yourself. The world changes. You have to change," former Itaú Unibanco CEO Roberto Setúbal advises.

The same is true for your own leadership effectiveness. As BlackRock CEO Larry Fink says, "One of the most important characteristics of a good leader is knowing your weaknesses and admitting them." To achieve this self-knowledge, successful CEOs find great benefit in getting an outsider's perspective. Chevron's Wirth undergoes periodic 360-degree reviews that gather feedback from board members, his team, and managers below his direct reports. When looking at this extensive feedback, Wirth asks, "What are the real messages here? And what are the things that I need to change that are the most important?" Such assessments, he says, "allow you to understand yourself and others, and how you interact with others. They create a framework for conversation about behavior and preferences and can give you a vehicle to get any baggage out on the table."

The results of doing so can be game-changing. "In year six of my eleven-year journey," Intuit's Smith explains, "my 360-degree feedback came back with, 'Brad is lowering the standards in the company because he's being too kind in reviews and isn't willing to call anybody out. He has this philosophy of praising in public and coaching in private, but it's robbing the rest of us of knowing where his standard of quality really is.'" Knowing the company needed him to be different, Smith changed his approach. "I challenged myself to be kind to the person but tough on the issue, and everyone in the company knew it," he says. "I told people, 'Keep me true to this, if you don't think I'm being concrete enough about whether the work is good enough. But I also want you to know that I'm not out to embarrass people.'"

## Collaboratively Define the Next S-Curve

Between three and five years into their tenure, the best CEOs typically take what they've learned and, thinking like an outsider, create the next performance S-curve for their company. The concept of the S-curve is that, for any strategy, there's a period of slow initial progress as the strategy is formed and initiatives are launched. This is followed by a rapid ascent from the cumulative effect of initiatives coming to fruition, and then by a plateau where the value of the portfolio of strategic initiatives has largely been captured. Aligning and mobilizing the organization to drive toward the next level of performance isn't easy, as JPMorgan Chase's Dimon explains: "Companies are always slowing down, always getting more bureaucratic. Even great people who don't intend to slow things down tend to do this," he says. "You have to constantly fight to improve." Dominic Barton, McKinsey's former global managing partner, uses a powerful analogy for the intensity of effort required: "No one likes change, so you need to create a rhythm of change. Think of it as applying 'heart paddles' to the organization."

Brian Moynihan describes his experience moving Bank of America from one S-curve to another: "Early on, our goal was to be the most admired company in the world. There's nothing wrong with that. That's defined by your customers, your shareholders, your teammates, and your communities," he states. "But then we needed to find a way to grow faster." This meant setting new goals for the company and employing a new mindset. "We flipped the question from 'What do our stakeholders want from us?' to 'What would we like the power to do for them?' This was a flip from looking outward, to looking inward and empowering our employees."

Some CEOs will choose to stay on and lead their company through multiple S-curves during their time at the helm. During Setúbal's twenty-two-year tenure at Brazil's Itaú Unibanco, he led the company through four S-curves. In his first act, he turned Banco Itaú from a regional to a national bank by quickly acquiring and integrating four large and troubled state-owned banks. In his second act, he invested heavily to move the bank from being retail-only, to being a leader in corporate and investment banking, as well as expanding into wealth management and into three other Latin American countries. In his third act, he implemented an agile operating model, radically reduced overhead, increased efficiency, overhauled the company's performance culture, and negotiated and executed a merger with Unibanco. In his final act, he aggressively drove growth in Brazil, pushed further Latin American expansion, and prioritized investments to digitalize the bank.

While CEOs should clearly define the next S-curve, they'd be well-advised not to simply dictate it to their organization and expect it to get done. The best leaders, consciously or instinctively, understand the need to get others involved in shaping the plan. This lesson is powerfully illustrated by another Kahneman social experiment. In this one, Kahneman ran a lottery with a twist.[8] Half the participants were randomly assigned a numbered lottery ticket. The remaining half were given a blank ticket and a pen and asked to choose their own lottery number. Just before drawing the winning number, the researchers offered to buy back all the tickets. They wanted to find out how much they'd have to pay people who wrote down their own number compared with people who were handed a random number.

The rational expectation would be that there should be no difference in how much the researchers had to pay people. After all, a lottery is pure chance. Every number, whether chosen or assigned, should have the same value because it has the same probability of being the winner. The answer, however, is predictably irrational. Regardless of nationality, demographic group, or the size of the prize, people who wrote their own lottery ticket number demanded at least five times more than the others for their tickets. This reveals an important truth about human nature. As Medtronic's George puts it, "People support what they help create." The underlying psychology relates to our desire for control, which is a deep-rooted survival instinct. Tapping into the "lottery ticket effect" takes time, but the return is high, as former Adidas CEO Herbert Hainer discovered. He adopted a collaborative approach to shaping the final S-curve in his tenure. "It took us five months," he shares, "but [the process] unleashed enormous spirit, new ideas, and creativity."

Virtually every successful CEO we spoke to has taken a collaborative—not a "thou shalt"—approach to defining their company's next S-curve. Late in his tenure, for example, Maurice Lévy, the CEO of multinational advertising and PR goliath Publicis, realized that his acquisition-led growth strategy had largely played itself out. It was time for another S-curve. Even though he had a clear view of what needed to be done, he captured the lottery ticket effect by engaging his executive team and the next level of management—roughly three hundred veteran leaders plus fifty recently promoted managers under the age of thirty—in a multi-month process to take Lévy's view, refine it, and make it their own. Executives worked in subgroups where ideas for the future of Publicis were debated, combined, and prioritized. Ultimately, what emerged was an S-curve dubbed "the Power of One" that focused on serving customers through cross-functional teams.

Great CEOs also understand that creating the next S-curve isn't just about setting strategy. Driving change requires pulling all the levers available. For example, at PepsiCo, Laguarta's mid-tenure pivot didn't just include portfolio transformation and digitalization; it was also organizational in nature. "We made the big decision to integrate our North American beverage and food businesses," he shares. "That had been hotly debated for many years and, when we finally did it, it sent ripples across the organization, even internationally."

Laguarta also rotated more than 50 percent of his senior team into other positions. Doing so was particularly challenging. "People wonder why you're changing leaders who seem to be doing a great job," he reflects. "They don't yet see that you are thinking about the next chapter and recognize that, if you don't do it, you're not doing the best for the company." Making such moves with each S-curve also ensures that, even under a long-tenured CEO, room is made for new opportunities for up-and-coming talent.

Often the most difficult and powerful lever to drive change mid-tenure is to adjust your own leadership style. BlackRock's Fink puts it succinctly: "If you're going to be successful, you have to transform yourself." For example, Adobe's Shantanu Narayen realized mid-tenure that he should be more directive: "I recognized that my job isn't just facilitating; it's making the final call on the big issues so we can move forward." For Best Buy's Hubert Joly, the mid-tenure shift was in the opposite direction. He went from "making a lot of the decisions" during the turnaround S-curve to "pushing decision-making down" during the next, more growth-oriented phase. After the turmoil of the global financial crisis, Bank of America's Moynihan realized mid-tenure that he had to do a better job of being strategic. "I had to learn to walk and chew gum," he says. "I had to execute day to day, but I also had to always be looking farther into the future."

## Future-Proof the Organization

Four years into his tenure as Boeing CEO, Dennis Muilenburg was named *Aviation Week*'s Person of the Year 2018. Eleven months later, his board asked him to step down amid the company's 737 MAX debacle. Three and a half years after being named CEO of BP, Tony Hayward resigned in the aftermath of the Deepwater Horizon oil spill. Unfortunately, "from adulation to resignation" is a CEO narrative that plays out all too often.

When things are going well, it's hard to imagine that an existential crisis could be looming. Unfortunately, no matter how well a company is run, the question for even the best CEOs isn't whether they'll have to lead through a crisis, but when. From 2010 to 2017, for example, headlines that carried the word "crisis" alongside the names of the 100 largest companies on Forbes Global 2000 appeared 80 percent more often than in the previous decade.[9] Says NYU Langone Health's Dr. Robert Grossman, "One of the things about being a CEO that nobody tells you is that, if you stay there long enough, you're going to have a number of crises. During my eighteen years, we've had four major crises."

A crisis can arise from anywhere. It may be sparked by high-profile media coverage of a passenger sustaining injuries while being dragged from an overbooked plane, as then CEO and later executive chair of United Airlines Oscar Munoz experienced. Or it may come after a widespread cyber breach, as Richard Smith, former CEO of the credit agency Equifax, found out. It may stem from a costly safety issue, an ethical conduct problem, a hostile takeover attempt—the possibilities are endless. Not all crises are company specific. Macroeconomic events, pandemics, international conflicts, natural disasters, social conflicts, terrorist attacks, and countless other external factors can all create crisis conditions for CEOs.

A crisis can end a CEO's otherwise great tenure, or it can be deftly harnessed to propel a company to new levels of postcrisis performance. Those who achieve positive outcomes recognize that the best time to prepare for a crisis is never on the day of the crisis itself. Instead, they regularly stress-test their business to make sure they're ready to go when a crisis comes. Chevron's Wirth explains why such stress-testing is useful: "Even if you run drills, you never are going to anticipate the black swan. But what you do is you start to build muscle memory for asking the right questions and for thinking about the collateral impacts that are very difficult to identify in the heat of the moment." This doesn't mean such exercises will be popular. "Writing business continuity plans is a demanding process, but the preparation and practice is absolutely critical, which is why it must be a CEO priority," advises Nasdaq's Adena Friedman.

At Bank of America, Moynihan explains: "We're always doing what we call 'risk identification.' Where are the issues, and where aren't they? What do we think about them? And how do we address them?" At Merck, Ken Frazier describes, "We did tabletop exercises around critical risks, such as patients being hurt in clinical trials or by counterfeit drugs. During a cyberattack, a team of people was ready to swing into action, and we didn't miss a beat." At Netflix, Reed Hastings ran an exercise that poses this problem: "It's ten years out, and Netflix is a failed firm. What are the different causes?" Hastings and his team worked through the list, making assessments of the respective probabilities. "Sometimes the discussion turned to what we can do about some of these risks," he says, "but many times, just defining what risks we faced prompted people to adjust behavior in smart ways that made us more resilient."

Relationships with stakeholders should also be stress-tested. As GM's Mary Barra puts it, "Relationships with our stakeholders—governments, dealers, suppliers, unions, and communities—aren't a 'nice to do.' They're part of running the company well." It's important to build goodwill with key groups over time, so that if and when a crisis happens, you're considered innocent until proven guilty instead of the other way around. As S&P Global's Peterson reminds us: "You need to build relationships in the good times. You can't just show up when there's a problem and say, 'Oh, please help me.' They may say, 'Well, who are you?'"

A good crisis playbook lays out the leadership protocols, control tower configuration, action plans, and communication approaches for when a crisis hits. Such plans shouldn't be timid, as IBM's Krishna explains. "An important question is how do you very quickly engage with a crisis? This is something which almost all CEOs are advised not to do. They're told, 'Oh no, don't engage. It's going to be ugly. It'll tarnish your reputation.' That's not the best approach. If you don't engage, it's going to get even worse." Crisis playbooks shouldn't simply triage problems; they can also contemplate what upside can be captured. Krishna continues, "You can say, 'Let's plan for the minimum possible dip.' Or you can say, 'If we're going to make changes anyway, let's do all the things we were going to do in the next two and a half years in the next three months.'" In the words of Adobe's Narayen, "A crisis is a terrible thing to waste!"

The playbook should also define the leading indicators of an escalating threat and how they can be measured. Some crises, such as the COVID-19 pandemic, are easier to identify than others. "One secret about crisis management is recognizing when you have one," General Mills' Powell shares. "A crisis can come from a very committed start-up that is about to beat you. You've got to be on the lookout for those companies that have a thousand rabid users. Let it grab your attention, and then react early, or you won't see the crisis coming." Vista Equity's Robert Smith points out the importance of having diverse points of view in the mix to help determine what is a genuine threat and what isn't: "Invariably somebody's going to figure out some way to introduce some risk that you've never experienced before, and you need a diversity of thought and capabilities to render judgments on this data and information."

Future-proofing also means actively building the strength of your company's talent bench. It's important to put real time and energy into coaching, retention, performance management, and succession planning for the most value-creating roles—the most important being your own. In the next chapter, we will explore succession planning in more depth, but it's important to start thinking about it well before you reach the final stage of your tenure. "Don't let succession planning sneak up on you," advises Intuit's Smith. "Grooming successors takes time, and your brand will be as much about what happens two or three years after you leave as when you were in." The best CEOs typically discuss succession planning with their board once or twice a year. S&P Global's Peterson describes his regular conversations with his board on the topic: "The real emphasis was: What sort of talent do we need to enable our strategy? How can we continue to help our people grow and learn? Who's getting ready to be the next CEO, and how can we support them?"

Finally, during your mid-tenure years, you need to think about future-proofing yourself. As he entered the middle years, Merck's Frazier realized that, "To be honest, the job was exhausting. I started to see my energy ebb." By carving out more time to stay in shape and connect with family, he was able to stay recharged on the road ahead. Beyond your physical health and that of your relationships outside of work, it's also important to stay aware of the extent to which your sense of self-worth and identity has become tied up in the role, as there will inevitably come a day when, in the words of U.S. Bancorp's Richard Davis, "People don't laugh at your jokes, and they don't call anymore."

IDB's Lilach Asher-Topilsky used a daily ritual to help her stay grounded throughout her tenure: "Every morning, when I went to my office, I entered the room, looked at my chair, and reminded myself that people were going to walk in and talk to the chair. I sit in this chair now, but I have to remember that I have to be humble. I have to remember that everyone is the same. I sit in this chair, and it makes me powerful, but tomorrow I'm not going to be in this chair."

---

By the time the hare in Aesop's fable wakes up, it's too late. Unlike the hapless hare, the best mid-tenure CEOs don't become complacent when they're winning. They remain as bold and focused as they were at the starting line, and they dig even deeper to succeed on the road ahead.

They enhance their learning, take an outsider's perspective toward their business, collaboratively define new S-curves, and future-proof their organizations in such a way that they not only maintain their lead but extend it. In keeping with the universal truths of Aesop's Fables, these lessons also apply in many other leadership situations. As such, we hope these insights from CEOs will help leaders at all levels achieve sustained success throughout their tenure.

*The greatness of our lives is not in what we leave behind, but in what we send forward.*

—RAY NOAH

CHAPTER FOUR
# Sending It Forward: Successfully Transitioning Out of the CEO Role

One of the most exciting athletic contests in the Summer Olympic Games is the 4x100-meter relay race. The event, which was inspired by ancient Greek couriers handing "message sticks" to one another, was introduced at the Stockholm Olympics in 1912. For the entirety of the twentieth century, the US team dominated the event. Not once in the twenty-first century, however, has the US team brought home a gold medal, despite many of its members having done so in their individual events.

What's the problem? Simple: bad handoffs. Consider *New York* magazine's description of one such handoff at the 2020 Tokyo Olympics: "As the pair attempted to pass the baton, they looked more like Keystone Cops than two of the five fastest men in the world."[1] As a result, the team failed to even advance to the final. At the same time, when well-synchronized handoffs happen, relay times are typically two to three seconds faster than the sum of the best times of individual runners.

When you're a celebrated CEO who has successfully led a company through multiple cycles of performance improvement, it's hard to imagine looking like a Keystone Cop at the end of your career as you pass the baton. Yet as the transition gets closer, the reality that you've never actually done a CEO handover before can feel daunting. Unlike Olympic athletes who practice their handoff timing, pacing, technique, and communication over and over with the grandstands empty, you'll only have one very public shot at it, and you'll be doing so while under emotional strain. As Caterpillar's former CEO Jim Owens puts it, "In the end, the hardest part of the CEO role is leaving."

The best CEOs are less worried about how their own reputation might fare in the transition, and more focused on how the change will impact the institution moving forward. HCA Healthcare's Sam Hazen describes the goal of the handover: "If you're successful in the relay race, you're not dropping the baton. And not just that; you're also setting up the next runner to be better and go faster than you did in your leg of the race." Dropped batons, on the other hand, exact a huge cost. In S&P 1500 companies, poorly managed CEO and C-suite transitions wipe out close to $1 trillion in market value every year.[2]

Microsoft CEO Satya Nadella stresses the importance of taking an institutional view of transitions: "My dad, a civil servant in India, always used to talk about institution builders as those people whose successors do better than they did themselves. I love that definition. I feel that if the next CEO of Microsoft can be even more successful than I am, then maybe I've done my job right. If the next CEO of Microsoft crashes and burns, that may result in a different verdict."

While the specifics of every transition differ depending on the circumstances, it's recommended that any CEO who's excelled in the role but senses it's time to start thinking about the endgame do the following:

- Firmly decide when to go.
- Finish the job of preparing successors.
- Hand over gracefully.
- Embrace what's next.

## Firmly Decide When to Go

Some CEOs enter the job with a clear idea of how long they want to stay, as was the case with CCHMC's Michael Fisher: "When I started the role, I told the board that if I'm healthy and stakeholders think I'm doing a good job, I'll do this for, give or take, ten years." In Fisher's case, he ended up staying almost twelve, which is a bit longer than the 11.2 years the highest-performing CEOs on average spend in the role. For all large-company CEOs, tenures are far shorter: just 7.3 years.

Getting the timing right for your departure is vital. Like fine wine, you'll have become better at your role with time and experience—but at some point, there'll be an inevitable decline. There are many warning signs that this is happening to a CEO. On one end of the spectrum, it's when the desire to protect their reputation of making quarterly numbers causes them to shy away from making bold moves and investments in the future. On the other end, it's when late-tenured CEOs whose strategies have played out become desperate to avoid a growth slowdown and opt to make large, complex acquisitions that are unlikely to be accretive for the institution. Beneath such moves often lurks a selfish desire to soothe increasing anxiety, unrest, and potentially even boredom.

The best chief executives know that there's no place for ego in determining when to go; what matters is what's best for the institution. Often there's a natural need for the company to pivot in a new direction, but the sitting CEO isn't the best one equipped to lead the transition. Gail Kelly chose to leave the Australian bank Westpac when she felt her customer-centric strategy was well in place and she had a successor ready who'd be better suited to lead the company into a more digital future. Sony's Kazuo Hirai felt that, while he was the right person to transform the company, he was less suited for the more stable phase to follow.

While the experience of others is instructive, knowing when to step down is a very personal, and difficult, decision. "It's hard to know when the right time to leave is," shares former Goldman Sachs CEO Lloyd Blankfein. "When times are tougher, you can't leave. And when times are better, you don't want to leave." Subsequent to his tenure at the helm of Medtronic, Bill George taught Harvard Business School classes that focused on the arc of a CEO's tenure. He suggests that CEOs regularly ask themselves the following questions to know when the time is right:

- Do you still find fulfillment and joy?

- Are you continuing to learn and feel challenged?

- Are there new personal circumstances that you should be taking into account (for example, family or personal health issues)?

- Are there unique opportunities outside that won't come around again?

- How is succession shaping up? (Is more time needed to prepare someone? Are you blocking someone who can lead the next era?)

- Are there company-specific milestones that make transitioning out more or less natural (such as the integration of a major acquisition, the launch of an important new product, or the completion of a long-running project)?

- Is the industry changing so dramatically that the company would benefit from a new perspective?

- Are you staying primarily because you can't imagine what comes next?

With these considerations in mind, the best CEOs clarify and commit to a time frame with their board well in advance of their planned departure date. "Without a clear timetable," says George, "grooming internal successors and following an orderly succession process become challenging." Typically, the lead time given is at least two years.

Ultimately, the adage "It's always better to drink wine a year early than a day too late" also applies to CEO succession. As Intuit's Brad Smith explains: "I had friends who stayed a couple of years too long in the job. I thought to myself, 'My gosh, how could they not have seen this coming?' Then I thought about all the athletes that stay one or two years past their prime. And you think, 'Man, I don't want to be that.' The only question you have to ask yourself is if you want to be the one choosing the date, or you want someone else to choose it for you."

## Finish the Job of Preparing Successors

In a successful relay, the person receiving the baton starts running well before the baton reaches them. The same can be said for succession planning. Although ultimately the job of hiring and firing the CEO rests with the board, the best chief executives work with their directors on succession planning throughout their tenure to ensure there are runners who have the momentum to receive the handoff. "Bill Campbell [Intuit's chair and coach to many Silicon Valley CEOs] helped me," says Intuit's Smith. "The first day I was in the job as CEO, he told me, 'I want you not to think of succession planning as replacing yourself. I want you to think about it as leadership development of your team. We're okay if we groom CEOs and—because you're not ready to leave or we don't want you to leave—they go someplace else. Because then Intuit will simply be known as a leadership factory.'"

Heeding this advice, Smith gave a verbal update on his succession plan to his board every quarter during his tenure, and once a year the company would have an official succession planning session facilitated by an outside consulting firm. In this session, the criteria for the next CEO were updated as the company's needs changed or as the markets shifted. The board also formally reviewed the pipeline of both internal and external candidates. Smith concludes, "Ultimately, we talked about succession forty-four times in my eleven years before the board made the decision, and that ensured there were no surprises such as, 'You think you groomed a successor; we don't agree.'"

It also pays to get your head of human resources intimately involved in this process. At DBS Bank, for example, Piyush Gupta says, "For every job, mine included, we [my head of HR and I] work through the slate—who could do the job soon, and who could do the job in three or five years? We then case manage a hundred-odd people. Who needs to move, where should we move them, and how do we get them the exposure and growth they need to get from point A to point B? It's very well structured."

When it comes time for a transition, if you've engaged your board and head of human resources the way Smith and Gupta did, the board will have clarity on both what attributes are needed and who the best internal candidates are. Caterpillar's Owens puts it starkly: "At any large company, shame on them if they don't have at least three strong candidates to take over the top job." IBM's Arvind Krishna shares the complexity of doing so: "Sometimes boards form an opinion. Sometimes the public forms an opinion. Sometimes people get sick. Lots of things can happen. So I think you always have to be prepared for a transition. As CEO, it's part of my job to prepare enough successors."

If the process isn't well managed, succession planning can lead to unpleasant cultural dynamics. "You might not intend to set up a horse race, but it inevitably becomes one," Westpac's Kelly observes. There are ways to mitigate office politics, however. Kelly's approach was straightforward. "I had an explicit conversation with the candidates who were in the running to let them know their behavior would be watched," she says. "I was clear with them. I said, 'You can't allow your teams to play politics in any shape or form, and neither can you. You must support every member of the team to be the best they can be.' That worked superbly well." Kelly adds, "I also had to treat them equally, not playing any favorites, and they trusted I would [do that]." It's also important not to make any promises to candidates during the process. Ultimately, the decision belongs to the board.

So what does the endgame of succession planning look like? Adobe's Shantanu Narayen shares his approach: "Retirement isn't a subject that should be avoided. You should be asking yourself, how am I giving people the opportunity to continue to grow their impact on the business? Am I giving potential successors all the things I was fortunate enough to get—an opportunity to understand the entire business—and not pigeonholing them? My attitude is, whether they want to be on a board or on earnings calls, doing press or doing investor relations—allow them those opportunities."

In some cases, it also makes sense to move potential successors into new roles to further elevate their profile in the lead-up to a passing of the baton. As was pointed out earlier in this book, though, taking a new job so late in the race can do more harm than good, because in all likelihood there's not enough time for a leader to establish themselves and excel in a new role. In the last year or two of a CEO's tenure, it's better to develop candidates by involving them in enterprise-level projects, committees, and coaching programs.

The CEO's role in succession planning ends once they've helped the board determine the right criteria and develop a list of internal candidates. It's then up to the board to interview candidates and involve outside parties in the decision (for instance, headhunting firms and interview panels that include sitting executives). "You have to have a legitimate search process, and it has to be fair, because otherwise the person who's chosen will always be diminished in the eyes of everybody," explains NYU Langone Health's Dr. Robert Grossman. "That's why you have search committees. I will do my very best to make the next person successful, but I'm not commenting on anyone, because if I say one word, it could taint the process."

The "finish the job" notion, of course, doesn't just apply to succession planning. We've seen some CEOs take their foot off the gas once they've decided that it's time to go. Given that the time between when you notify the board of your intention to leave and when the board names your successor is a matter of years, the institution can lose some of its competitive edge if the sitting CEO doesn't stay focused to the very end. It may sound obvious, but as former Cadence Design Systems CEO Lip-Bu Tan shares, "A lot of temptations can derail you. You have to stay focused on the things that really matter."

## Hand Over Gracefully

Once a successor is chosen by the board, it's time to make the actual handoff happen. In track and field, success means passing the baton to the next runner in such a way that they can easily grasp it and take it forward rapidly without letting it drop. Successful CEO handovers have similar attributes.

Let's start with how you can make the baton easy to grasp. The first thing you'll need to do is explain to the new CEO that they don't need to be you; the board chose them because of their own special skills and attributes and because they're the best fit for the institutional road ahead. "That's one of the most important things—to not try to create another version of yourself," shares Elevance Health's Gail Boudreaux. "The reality is, whoever it is, that person is going to be completely different. And you want that. The board has to pick not based on what they like about you but based on what they want the company to be going forward and what skill sets the leader will therefore need."

Another way you can make things easier for your successor is to give them the gift of resolving any unpleasant but institutionally important decisions before the handoff. "You'll have some unassailable capital as a successful outgoing CEO," explains CCHMC's Fisher. "Use it to address some of the lingering tough issues, be they people issues or otherwise, so that your successor doesn't have any messes to clean up." At the same time, Fisher advises not going too far. "If there are important strategic hires and/or strategic decisions to be made, if at all possible let your successor get their fingerprints on those decisions. They'll be the one living with them."

You want your successor to move forward rapidly, but too fast a handoff could create instability, and too slow could mean you're getting in the way. In track and field, handoffs happen in the twenty-meter "exchange zone," inside which the next runner must receive the baton from the current runner. The exchange zone for a CEO transition is typically six to nine months and sequenced in three stages:

- **Stage one:** Once your successor is announced, you'll still largely run the company for two to three months to give them time to do their listening tour and sharpen their thoughts on how they want to run the company. During this time, you'll also give them full exposure to what the role entails, share the rationale behind past decisions, discuss strengths and weaknesses of the top team and the organization at large, and warmly hand off important stakeholder relationships (for example, large customers, investors, regulators, suppliers, and community leaders). This is also when you can offer your successor some "live, with a safety net" learning opportunities (roles in senior staff meetings, town halls, board meetings, et cetera) so they can get a good feel for what it means to sit in the driver's seat.

- **Stage two:** In the two to three months leading up to your successor's formal start date, you two become copilots. During this time, as Intuit's Smith describes, "any decision that impacts the next few months, the sitting CEO should take. If it's got longer-term implications that the successor will have to live with—such as a restructure or major engineering effort—the successor should take it." In this stage, it's important that you shift from a teaching and enabling stance to a supporting one. More than anything, you're encouraging your followers to accept and embrace their new leader.

- **Stage three:** After the formal start date, all decision-making is transferred to your successor, and your job is simply to be available for counsel or practical support as directed by them. This typically involves moving your office to a new location away from headquarters. This is also a time when you should let yourself and your career be celebrated—not out of vanity, but because of how important such closure is for others both individually and institutionally. "Over my last sixty days in the role, I went to virtually every significant area of the medical center," recounts CCHMC's Fisher. "It was a chance for me to thank them and for them to reminisce with me, and it was such important closure for all of us."

Before you start the handoff, it's important to have an explicit upfront conversation with your successor to jointly shape how decision-making will shift over time, and to create a concrete plan for how the process will work. It's also important to be explicit about what happens after the handoff is complete.

In many companies, the outgoing CEO is asked to take on an executive chairman role. The idea is well-intentioned: keep the experience of the former CEO and combine it with the fresh ideas and vigor of the new CEO. In practice, staying around generally isn't a good idea. After all, new CEOs should want to reframe what winning looks like, make bold moves early and often, and dynamically reallocate resources—all of which runs counter to the inertia created by having the old guard still in a leadership role. Research backs this notion: A new CEO's early dismissal is 2.4 times more likely when the outgoing CEO remains the board chair. *The Wall Street Journal* memorably drove home the point in saying, "Imagine if the former president moved out of the Oval Office but still lived in the White House."[3]

"You really need to get out of the way," suggests Caterpillar's Owens, "and let your successor critique what you did and talk about what needs to go way better." Intuit's Smith concurs: "The last step is to celebrate your successor's success. There's nothing worse than the Ghost of Christmas Past commenting on whether a leader is doing everything the way they should." Smith holds this view despite having successfully played the executive chairman role at Intuit. "Honestly, in hindsight, I should have just stepped away," he says. "That's not because we had any dynamic tension. I simply think it's better to exit and let the CEO do their thing."

This isn't to say that there aren't some situations that warrant exceptions to this line of thinking—for example, where the board has skipped over a leadership generation to advance a talented but "green" up-and-comer for the role, or where the incumbent CEO has been deeply involved in a not-yet-completed acquisition or integration.

## Embrace What's Next

Stepping down from a powerful job can be very difficult. As former US president Harry Truman said shortly after leaving office, "Two hours ago I could have said five words and been quoted in every capital of the world. Now I could talk for two hours, and nobody would give a damn." Westpac's Kelly highlights the emotional impact of having to move on: "For a lot of people, it's 'I am what I do, and I do my job.' That's where their relevance and purpose come from. And that's really hard to leave." There can also be compounding emotional challenges. As former Xerox CEO Anne Mulcahy shares, "By the time you're at retirement age, your kids have left home too. It's double retirement."

We advise CEOs to acknowledge, directly confront, and overcome the basic human fears and needs that arise when stepping down. These include losing the relevance, power, attention, and admiration that come with the job, and suddenly finding yourself spending time at home with a partner who has established their own rhythms and independent priorities. Add into the mix the term "retirement," which to some implies that the ravages of age and physical decline are accelerating—all of which can be mentally and emotionally difficult to embrace.

While transitions can be traumatic, that stress is more than counterbalanced by the feeling of liberation brought by stepping down. Any sense of loss is typically short-lived as it becomes clear that life can be even more vibrant, interesting, and fulfilling when you're freed of the constraints of the corporate calendar. You can invest more in personal relationships and use your experience to make a difference in many spheres. "A good time to step down," shares former ICICI Bank CEO KV Kamath, "is when you see you can do a lot more exciting things outside than you sense you can do within the organization." Seeing such opportunities is often easier after some very long-term-oriented reflection. PepsiCo's Ramon Laguarta explains, "We can think we're bigger than life, but we're not. One day we're not going to be around and it's important to be grounded in what you want it to say on your gravestone—the legacy you'll leave beyond what you did for your company."

The best CEOs don't just confront their emotions upon departure; they also make plans to avoid what Ken Chenault, former CEO of American Express, describes as "falling into the abyss." "Don't ignore it. It's very important to be thoughtful about life after being the CEO." Practically speaking, that means that before leaving the role, you should identify what's important to you. In Chenault's case, even though he didn't know precisely what he'd be doing, he says, "When opportunities came my way, I was ready, because I had thought about them."

Following Chenault's advice to identify what's important to you, Intuit's Smith reflected on what he was going to miss about his role as CEO. "I was going to miss the jersey that made me part of a team and the opportunities to develop the next generation of leaders, and I was going to miss having a scoreboard to measure success by," he reveals. "Then I put my energy not in what I was leaving behind, but in what the next thing could be that would have those characteristics. I was running toward something, rather than walking away from something."

Whatever your interests, as a successful former CEO, you'll be able to find ample opportunities in your new life. For those of a certain age, being CEO of another company may be in the cards. Others may simply want to retire to a quieter life focused on family, friends, and leisure. Between those bookends, however, are myriad options: advisor, investor, board member, entrepreneur, politician, public servant, philanthropist, teacher, and so on. In Smith's case, he became the president of Marshall University in his home state of West Virginia. "Now I wake up every morning wearing a jersey, helping the next generation, and knowing from the scoreboard if we're moving the ball forward," he beams. "I'm 100 percent in."

For most, the path to the next act will start with some experimentation, the seeds for which can be planted before stepping out of the CEO role. "I wanted to start with a portfolio of activities," CCHMC's Fisher explains, "so I started putting some pieces in place—a little bit of business, a little bit of civic and philanthropic work, and some plans with family—so that when I finished, I'd have some ways to contribute, even if it wasn't a full slate." It's important to keep in mind that the first opportunities that come your way may not be the best ones, and it's easy for your life to feel fragmented owing to too many smaller commitments prompted by the self-created pressure to keep busy. It typically takes up to a year of experimenting with a targeted portfolio before it becomes clear where you should commit to bigger, longer-term involvement.

If you have a significant other, the exploration of what's important to you and the shaping of your post-CEO portfolio is something best done together. Doing so creates a deeper connection in the near term and helps mitigate frustrations down the road. If they've been waiting patiently for you to retire so you can travel the world together and that's not something on your radar, it's important to have those conversations up front. ASML's Peter Wennink notes what can happen otherwise: "It can be a problem. My wife tells me, 'Peter, you have a completely different definition of retirement than I have. You have to stop doing so much!'" A third party can sometimes be helpful in facilitating such conversations.

Medtronic's George reports, "My wife, Penny, and I met with a counselor six months before I left Medtronic to discuss those issues, and we were able to address the different stages we were at in our careers."

Ultimately, being CEO is just one chapter in the story of your life. As you embark on your next chapter, the adage that "failing to plan is planning to fail" applies. At the same time, it's wise not to hold too tightly to such plans, as though they were a corporate transformation project. Be open to serendipity, knowing that the most exciting opportunities will sometimes come from the most unexpected sources. Also remember that the traits of continuous learning, boldness, authenticity, and service leadership that have underpinned success in the previous chapters of your life will continue to serve you well.

---

Great CEOs ultimately see themselves as part of an ongoing institutional relay race where each generation of leadership hands the next generation something better than they were themselves handed. By leaving at the right time and for the right reasons, helping the board find your replacement, ensuring a clean handoff to your successor, and knowing where you'll run to next, you'll achieve a gold medal–worthy finish to your CEO tenure.

> *Prediction is very difficult,*
> *especially about the future.*
> —NOBEL LAUREATE NIELS BOHR

CONCLUSION
# The Future of the CEO Role

The Beatles are by far the biggest-selling rock band of all time, with 600 million record sales worldwide. They are also routinely ranked as the number one or two rock band in history. According to *Forbes*, they are "to this day one of the most beloved acts in modern music, let alone rock music." Back in 1964, however, *National Review* founder William F. Buckley Jr. described them as "so unbelievably horrible, so appallingly unmusical, so dogmatically insensitive to the magic of the art, that they qualify as crowned heads of anti-music." Buckley wasn't the only skeptic. Decca Records rejected them after their 1962 audition, saying, "We don't like their sound, and guitar music is on the way out." Ray Bloch, musical director for *The Ed Sullivan Show*, said, "The only thing different is the hair, as far as I can see. I give them a year."

Clearly, predicting the future isn't easy. But as we discussed extensively in our prior book *CEO Excellence*, it's vital that CEOs have a well-defined point of view on where the world is going. With a differentiated perspective, leaders can place bets before new trends become conventional wisdom and maintain their convictions in spite of inevitable criticism. They also need to keep a level head and not get swept away by hype about markets that may not yet exist or technologies that may prove to be long shots. This ability to calibrate what matters most—and when and how to capitalize on it—has always been and will continue to be essential to succeeding as a CEO.

In this chapter, it's our turn to share our point of view on the future of the CEO role itself. Twenty years from now, will the four seasons as we've described them still be a helpful frame, and will the lessons we've shared for each still apply? To answer, we'll start by exploring the forces driving change, and reflect on their direction, magnitude, and causes. Equipped with that understanding, we then assert what future CEOs will be called upon to be and do differently (and what *not* to do—imagine how much more successful Decca Records would have been if they'd signed the Beatles!).

## The More Things Change . . .

As we write this book in early 2025, it feels to many like changes in the business world are happening faster and on a larger scale than ever. Consider that, whereas it took Facebook four and a half years to reach 100 million users and Instagram almost two and a half years,[1] ChatGPT recently did so in just two months.[2] Top-tier business publications such as *Harvard Business Review*, *Forbes*, and *Fortune* are rife with titles like "What It Takes to Lead Through an Era of Exponential Change," "The Unprecedented Pace of Change," "Navigating the Currents of Disruption,"[3] and "How to Thrive in an Era of Uncertainty."[4] Surveys of C-suite leaders show that they believe the rate of change affecting businesses is at an all-time high, and the majority expect it will accelerate.[5]

What are these extreme changes that are happening? To answer this question, we've surveyed much of the available literature and drawn on the expertise of our colleagues at McKinsey's Global Institute, the research arm of our firm that provides business and economic insights to help leaders make decisions. This helped us distill the major forces of change in today's business world, which fall into six categories:

- **Technology:** Today, over five billion people around the globe are plugged into the internet,[6] and the flow of data doubles every two years.[7] These numbers aren't just statistics—they represent a transformative shift in how we live, work, and interact with the world. The next wave of technological advancements promises to be even more groundbreaking. Artificial intelligence and machine learning, exemplified by tools like ChatGPT, are already redefining productivity and human-machine interaction. Blockchain technology, driving innovations like decentralized finance (DeFi), is reshaping our understanding of trust and value in a digital world. Meanwhile, fields like biotechnology—CRISPR and mRNA technologies, for example—are opening doors to new possibilities in medicine and genetics.

- **Global economic and geopolitical shifts:** The COVID-19 pandemic, still fresh in memory, exposed deep vulnerabilities in global supply chains and revealed just how fragile our interconnected systems are. The world order is now marked by severe realignments, as seen in rising tensions in US-China relations, the Russia-Ukraine war, and the ever-shifting dynamics of the Middle Eastern conflict. As we look forward, these shifts are poised to have a lasting impact on businesses on the global stage, influencing everything from trade and security to the very nature of international diplomacy.

- **Climate change and sustainability:** The reality of climate change is no longer a theoretical debate—it's a tangible crisis with devastating consequences. As climate change makes storms (from Hurricane Helene to Typhoon Yagi) more damaging and costly to businesses and economies, corporate leaders grapple with what commitments need to be made in relation to environmental, social, and governance (ESG) investments. Meanwhile, at the global level many governments are strengthening their climate commitments, enacting more robust policies and regulations, from carbon pricing mechanisms to stricter emissions standards.

- **Consumer behavior:** In the post–COVID-19 world, there has been a marked shift toward e-commerce and omnichannel experiences, which blend the convenience of online shopping with in-store visits. Digital payments such as Apple Pay have surged in popularity, as consumers seek faster, more secure ways to make transactions. At the same time, subscription models (streaming services, personal care products, pet supplies, et cetera) have become increasingly prevalent, offering convenience and personalized services that cater to our changing lifestyles. This new consumer landscape reflects a broader shift toward digitalization and convenience, with individuals prioritizing health, security, and seamless experiences in their purchasing habits.

- **Workforce and talent:** Spurred by the pandemic, remote collaboration tools like Zoom have become central to how we work. However, business leaders are still figuring out how to prevent remote work from becoming a three-day workweek. Further, the gig economy now fundamentally shapes how we shop and work, while automation continues to reshape industries. Globally, mental health support, workforce re-skilling, and diversity, equity, and inclusion (DEI) have all been important areas for corporate discussion and attention, often led by senior executives.

- **Demographic shifts:** We are witnessing mass migration from urban centers to suburban areas, alongside the resurgence of smaller cities as people seek more space and affordability. Climate change has also spurred migration, displacing communities in vulnerable areas. Compounding these changes, inequality has worsened in many countries, with disparities widening in health care, education, digital access, and economic opportunities (often to historic levels). In addition, the declining birth rate in many countries around the world is now below the replacement rate, calling into question the long-term viability of economic systems.

The sheer number and magnitude of variables in flux reinforces the argument that CEOs need to have a point of view on how these changes affect their short- and longer-term business outlooks. With every seismic shift comes a tremendous threat or an extraordinary opportunity, depending on when and how it's perceived and managed.

## ... The More Things Stay the Same

It's easy to see why terms such as "exponential," "uncertainty," "unprecedented," and "disruption" have become favorites among business leaders, thinkers, and other commentators. But is the level of uncertainty really greater now than it has been in the past? "History never repeats itself, but it often rhymes," Mark Twain supposedly said. We agree, and it strikes us that the assertion that things are changing faster than ever before may be more hyperbole than reality.

Let's look at a snapshot of what was in flux twenty years ago and compare it to the picture of today that we painted in the previous section. If we traveled by time machine to 2004, we would see that CEOs had just as much on their plate as they do today:

- **Technology:** The early 2000s kick-started the internet era. In 2004, the number of internet users had doubled over the previous three years—reaching nearly one billion globally and dramatically increasing the amount of data in the world. Company leaders were racing to build their digital capabilities. Smartphones, big data and machine learning, 3D printing, electric cars, flash drives, cloud computing, and augmented reality were all poised to vastly increase computing output and revolutionize the way we work and live.

- **Global economic and geopolitical shifts:** Although we tend to forget the past in the face of today's conflicts, 2004 was no cakewalk. The United States had recently endured a devastating terrorist attack on its own soil and was embroiled in two major wars, as it defended against a new "Axis of Evil." In the wake of the Enron scandal, one of the worst in US business history, the country's booming economy began to falter, sowing doubt and uncertainty among business leaders. Meanwhile, the European Union saw by far its largest expansion in history (known as the "big bang"), growing from fifteen to twenty-five countries and changing the shape of possibilities for business.[8]

- **Climate change and sustainability:** The news about climate change was no less dire twenty years ago than it is today. As one of the warmest years on record, 2004 was the year where scientific consensus on global warming became more established. The Pentagon formally reported on the dangers of "abrupt climate change," and the release of the blockbuster movie *The Day After Tomorrow* focused public discussion on the topic. That same year, the United Nations introduced the concept of environmental, social, and governance (ESG) measures, a clarion call to markets and CEOs to better integrate these factors into decision-making.

- **Consumer behavior:** Consumer trends have always shifted hard and fast. In the wake of the dot-com implosion, surviving e-commerce companies such as Amazon and eBay worked hard to attract customers with low prices and convenience. Consumers benefited from being able to research and compare prices of online products at a scale never seen before. Personalized marketing, customer loyalty programs, and customer reviews were being touted as transformational.

- **Workforce and talent:** Leaders were grappling with major changes in the employee landscape as the year marked the rise of the contingent workforce; an increased use of workforce analytics and metrics; the highest-ever demand for technical skills like programming, web development, and IT security; and a strong emphasis on building diverse workforces and promoting inclusive practices. The landmark legalization of same-sex marriage in Massachusetts highlighted the importance of considering sexual orientation in diversity initiatives as well.

- **Demographic shifts:** Many developed countries, such as Japan, Germany, and Italy, grappled with aging populations due to lower birth rates and longer life expectancy, posing challenges for economic growth and social welfare systems. This trend contrasted with developing nations, which were experiencing a youth bulge that created both opportunities and challenges in education and employment. At the same time, urbanization accelerated, particularly in developing countries, as people moved to cities in search of better economic opportunities. Immigration was also on the rise, driven by a mix of economic, political, and environmental factors.

Just as it appears there were as many variables in flux twenty years ago as there are today, we suspect twenty years from now the same observation will hold. This points to an important potential blind spot that today's leaders should be wary of—the generational exceptionalism fallacy. This occurs when those who are living in the "now" mistakenly believe that they are experiencing an unprecedented, high level of change. This misperception, in turn, leads people to ignore lessons and techniques from the past that could help them deal with the present and shape the future. We believe the risk of this bias affecting today's leaders is intensified by the media's tendency to dramatize current events.

The best CEOs recognize that history can be a powerful teacher and therefore don't succumb to this fallacy. Chevron's Michael Wirth is a great example of this. "We're a long-cycle industry, with leaders who've made capital investments that play out over decades and who have long-standing relationships with government leaders in countries around the world," he says. "These people have been through wars, pandemics, terrorist attacks, embargoes, boycotts, and sanctions—all things that have dramatically affected our company. Their insights and reflections on what they learned, what they wish they would've done differently, and what they think I should do today have been incredibly valuable to me. Without a line of communication to these advisors, you miss out on some of that continuity and history that can be so helpful."

This is why we believe that any discussion of how to lead into the future should start not with what is new, but with what has always been—and will continue to be—true. For that, we point our readers to the principles we laid out in our previous book, *CEO Excellence*. In it, we defined the six responsibilities of the CEO role that are timeless and structural. For each of these responsibilities we shared the mindset that has always and will continue to separate the best from the rest: 1) "being bold" in setting the direction, 2) "treating the soft stuff as the hard stuff" in aligning the organization, 3) "solving for the team's psychology" when mobilizing leaders, 4) "helping directors help the business" when engaging the board, 5) "starting with 'why?'" when connecting with stakeholders, and 6) "doing what only you can do" to maximize your personal effectiveness.

In our view, the CEO role will also always have a before, a beginning, a middle, and an end—the four seasons—as we have described. As such, in the future, CEO candidates will still be well-advised to gut check their motivations and expectations, elevate their perspective while boldly delivering results, round out their profile with humility, and understand the selection process and put their best foot forward. Those who start strong will continue to focus on building the institution (not oneself), listen and then act, nail their firsts, and play "big ball." The keys to staying ahead during the middle years as CEO will still be to enhance one's learning agenda, take an outsider's perspective, collaboratively define the next S-curve, and future-proof the organization. When passing the baton to the next CEO, the value of deciding when to go, finishing the job of preparing successors, handing the position over gracefully, and embracing what's next will remain vital.

To a large extent, applying the six mindsets and best practices across the four seasons enables leaders to both shape their environment and adapt to change, which is the sine qua non for leaders in any era. We now turn our sights from the more timeless advice on best practices to what we see as the most important "next practices" for the CEOs in the future.

## Next Practices

In the previous section we took the approach of using history to identify recurring patterns that can be applied in the future. An alternative approach, however, is to search for emergent variables from which the future can be extrapolated. In this approach, we've tried to spot future *possibilities*, or scenarios, that become more or less likely based on how each of these variables progresses.

Through this lens, we can see how the CEO's job has changed over time and can also look at today's variables to predict the future of the role. For example, the breakup of bloated organizations in the 1970s due to increased global competition elevated the importance of the shareholder and made shareholder rights a major focus of the CEO. The advent of cable TV news in the 1980s brought CEOs into the limelight, requiring them to focus more on their external image and communications. The technology revolution at the turn of the century ushered in a shift from physical to digital and intellectual assets, increasing the importance of the softer side of leadership. It also brought with it personal productivity enhancers such as the then-virtually ubiquitous BlackBerry, which simultaneously saved time and drained energy by creating the expectation that one had to be "on" 24/7. After the 2008 financial crisis, investors required boards to become more hands-on, which shifted the CEO's role in corporate governance. As social media usage became the norm in the last decade, the level of public scrutiny on the role has meant that CEOs have to more quickly and thoughtfully address stakeholder-related issues.

So how will this story continue to unfold? We've looked at the variables at play today, extrapolated a range of potential future scenarios, and then determined what we believe will be seven hallmarks of leaders who'll excel in the CEO role into the future:

1. **Leading through leaders.** Just five years ago, the largest companies in the world were on the cusp of achieving a trillion-dollar market cap. Now some are above three trillion. Despite technology advances, big corporations are adding to their headcounts as well. It used to be that major institutions might employ 100,000 people. Now they employ over a million. It's very conceivable that we'll see ten-trillion-dollar market cap companies with ten million employees in the not-too-distant future. At such an enormous scale, one wonders if a single person can possibly have all it takes to lead. As the Ancient Greek mathematician Archimedes put it: "Give me a lever long enough and a fulcrum on which to place it, and I shall move the world." CEOs of the future will find ways to gain leverage by "leading through leaders." In practice, what that means is that the best of the best in the future will turn their organizations into "leadership factories" where those in vital roles (on the order of hundreds) are both highly skilled and have robust succession plans, and where thousands of employees are equipped to be excellent problem-solvers both in value creation and risk management.

2. **Cultivating self-awareness.** Oliver Wendell Holmes Jr. once said of Franklin D. Roosevelt that he had a "second-class intellect but a first-class temperament." We believe this latter trait will become even more crucial for CEOs to succeed in the future. The ramped-up real-time scrutiny on

CEO decisions and behaviors will mean that the more grounded, adaptable, resilient, and purpose-driven one is, the more impact one will have. Those leaders who have a deep yet humble self-awareness of their energies, assumptions, effects on others, and a desire to grow over time possess a number of superpowers that others lack. One of these is a willingness to put trust in others to do the things they're expert at versus trying to control every variable. Another is the ability to be a stabilizing force amid rapid change by responding to situations creatively (in a display of "flow") versus reactively (in a display of "fight, flight, or freeze"), which in turn makes these leaders more adept at knowing when to absorb or amplify issues that emerge. Yet another superpower is a first instinct not to assign blame but, rather, to ask the question, "What am I doing that makes others respond this way and what can I do to create a better outcome?" A fourth superpower afforded by high self-awareness is the ability to connect with others on an emotional level, which can help motivate them to achieve the best results.

3. **Institutionalizing learning.** "Curiosity" was the answer given by Michael Dell when he was asked to name a single attribute that CEOs will need to succeed in the future. His answer echoes Albert Einstein's confession, "I have no special talent. I am only passionately curious." Having an inquisitive attitude has always been the hallmark of great CEOs, as it enables them to effectively challenge assumptions and connect dots across a multitude of variables and see opportunities that others don't. They lead with the question of "why?" to drive focus, and "why not?" to encourage boldness. In the future, the best CEOs will find ways to build this same muscle in their companies. This will involve institutionalizing internal learning through such mechanisms

as premortems and postmortems that give the organization a chance to pause, step back, and take stock of what's working, what isn't, what it means, and what to do about it. Institutionalizing external learning will be equally important. This may come in the form of periodic benchmarking or visits to companies both within and outside one's industry to learn best practices. For example, we've seen airlines improve their luggage handling systems by taking lessons from stock car racing pit crews. For the CEO, it will mean consistently asking expansive information gathering questions such as "What don't we know that we need to find out? What do we know now that we didn't a month ago? Who outside our walls are we learning from?"

4. **Being decisive.** Napoleon Bonaparte once observed, "Nothing is more difficult, and therefore more precious, than to be able to decide." The fact that companies that optimize for the whole are more successful—combined with the increasing size and complexity of large organizations—means it will become even more difficult and important for CEOs to make timely company-level optimization decisions. Consultative leadership will remain important (listening, collaborating, drawing out the opinions of others), but senior leaders must guard against any tendency toward "lowest common denominator" solutions where partial information and low consensus exists, as well as institutional inertia that leads to stagnation and bureaucracy. CEOs will need the fortitude to say "No" far more than "Yes" to their colleagues, regardless of whether such calls are popular. As Apple's former CEO Steve Jobs famously put it, "People think focus means saying yes to the thing you've got to focus on. But that's not what it means at all. It means saying no to the hundred other good ideas that are there."

5. **Making meaning.** Meaning has always been important. Over two thousand years ago Plato observed that humans are "beings in search of meaning." In recent times, the workplace has become an increasing source of identity and belonging for employees as time spent in traditional meaning-making settings such as family, community, and religious institutions has trended dramatically downward. We see this trend continuing. For a CEO, meaning-making involves motivating oneself and others from within—grounded in a deep-seated belief that "what I/we are doing matters." It's not about charisma and cheerleading—it's about engaging fully in one's own purpose and helping others connect with theirs. When the most senior leader acts with a sense of authentic purpose, they become more compelling as role models and more inspiring as communicators. They're able to connect with people both emotionally and intellectually, recognizing that not everyone draws meaning at work from the same sources. Research shows that the various sources include *oneself* (development, rewards, freedom), *fellow employees* (belonging, caring, fairness), *the company* (industry leadership, best practices, winning), *the customer* (providing a superior service or product), and *societal impact* (making the world a better place). The best meaning-makers ensure that their organization has a powerful reason *why* it does what it does on each of these five dimensions.

6. **Moral reasoning.** American civil rights activist Martin Luther King Jr. once asserted, "The time is always right to do what's right." While such wisdom is timeless, tomorrow's CEOs will need to put it into practice in answering many of humankind's most pressing and challenging ethical questions. The private sector is on the vanguard of determining how AI will be used or misused, what trade-offs will be made because of

geopolitical considerations, how short- versus long-term socioeconomic factors will be weighed, and what to do about looming environmental crises such as natural resource depletion, food chain contamination, and inhumane animal treatment. Decisions will have to be reached with a strong moral compass grounded in the axiom "Just because we can doesn't mean we should." Further, as with institutionalized learning, moral reasoning can't just be the responsibility of the CEO—it will need to permeate the organization. Beyond leading by example, chief executives will need to clearly communicate ethical standards; make ethics a priority in hiring, promotion, and rewards; foster a culture of openness; and teach people how to think critically about ethical issues.

7. **Embracing paradox.** F. Scott Fitzgerald's observation that "the test of a first-rate intelligence is the ability to hold two opposed ideas in the mind at the same time, and still retain the ability to function" will especially apply to future CEOs.

Consider these ten dichotomies that leaders will need to balance:

| CEOs need to do this... | While also doing this... |
| --- | --- |
| Deliver short-term results | Invest in long-term performance |
| Take time to gather facts and conduct analyses | Move fast to capture opportunities |
| Respect the past and create continuity | Disrupt the future |
| Maximize value for shareholders | Deliver positive impact for other stakeholders |
| Have the confidence to make tough calls | Have the humility to ask for and receive feedback |
| Build relationships with colleagues | Maintain enough distance to stay objective |

| CEOs need to do this... | While also doing this... |
| --- | --- |
| Pressure team members to put the organization first | Leverage the best of team members' individual skills |
| Get success-oriented people to risk failure | Get risk averse people to achieve extraordinary outcomes |
| Be in the most powerful position in the organization | Make others in the organization more powerful |
| Always give hope for the future | Confront the most brutal facts of their current reality |

These tensions will only become more pronounced going forward, and there are no easy answers. That said, the previously mentioned "next practices" of leading through leaders, cultivating self-awareness, institutionalizing learning, being decisive, making meaning, and moral reasoning will all enable CEOs of the future to embrace paradox effectively.

---

The act of predicting the future has a history. The good news is that it's one from which we can learn; the bad news is that we rarely do. By embracing the timeless truths about leadership at each stage of the journey, calibrating what matters most in the ever-changing business environment, and adopting leadership hallmarks that will correlate with success in all future scenarios, you'll be a CEO for all seasons—much to the delight of all stakeholders.

APPENDIX A:
# Reflection Exercises

In this section, we provide a selection of reflection exercises that McKinsey uses to counsel CEOs. We hope these will help you reflect on how some of the concepts we have explored together in this book apply to your situation. For each reflection, we provide a real-world example to illustrate the type of content that typically comes out of such discussions.

We've chosen to include these specific exercises because they apply across all four seasons of a CEO. In season one, they will help you prepare for your interviews with the board. Next, in season two, they will make it easier for you to align and mobilize your stakeholders. They are equally applicable as you define your next S-curve in season three. And, as you wind things down in season four, these reflections will help clarify what to look for and develop in your successor.

The six exercises we've chosen to cover are the following: direction setting, culture change, team performance, board effectiveness, stakeholder engagement, and personal leadership effectiveness. They are but a small sample of the full suite of reflection exercises we typically employ as we help CEOs achieve their full potential in each season, so that their organizations can then achieve their full potential as well.

## Reflection Exercise 1: Direction Setting

### WHY WE CHOSE THIS REFLECTION EXERCISE

American psychologist William Schutz observed, "Our understanding evolves in three phases: simplistic, complex, and profoundly simple." The goal of this reflection is to push your thinking on the vision and strategy of your organization into the "profoundly simple" zone. This, in turn, will make it far easier to align and mobilize your organization than if you emphasized only a simplistic "in a sentence" direction statement or, conversely, used a hundred-page strategy document to explain your company's direction.

### HOW IT SHOULD BE USED

Before going into this reflection, it's important to ground yourself in what's happening in the business environment with your customers, suppliers, competitors, substitutes, potential entrants, and so on. Then, once you understand that context, you'll need to determine where, when, and how to compete by creating or leveraging your competitive advantage. Once you choose a path forward, this exercise is designed to help you articulate the resulting direction in a way that's crisp, clear, and manageable.

It's often best to convene a small group of your closest advisors to tackle this exercise with you. Once you've formed a point of view on your strategy, your senior team will then improve upon it, taking ownership of the content. Then it's time for your communications team to put it in the context of a change story and sharpen and/or adjust the content for broad consumption (e.g., removing market-sensitive details that would be material information if shared publicly).

As you reflect, consider whether you have:

- Articulated a clear and compelling **vision** that reframes what winning looks like and significantly raises aspirations in a way the whole enterprise can own.

- Captured the essence of your strategy by creating a short list of **big moves** that will distance you from the competition (e.g., M&A, capital investment, productivity improvement, product and service differentiation).

- Made the strategy concrete and actionable by defining the specific **initiatives** needed for each big move and the related **measures of success.**

- Thought like an outsider as to what **resources** you will reallocate (e.g., dollars, people, attention) so you can focus on your highest priorities.

- Clarified what benefits all of the above will deliver to each of your **stakeholders**—which in turn will allow you to better inspire people and build conviction for your strategy.

## Reflection Exercise 1: Direction Setting (example)

| | | | | |
|---|---|---|---|---|
| **Where** are we headed? *(reframe the game vision)* | Move from #1 in our industry to be a top-quartile global industrial company | | | |
| **How** will we make it happen? *(big moves)* | Innovate high-margin products and services | Radically improve product profitability | Reshape the business portfolio | Build a high-performing organization |
| **What** actions will we take? *(initiatives)* | • Carve out a "new ventures" group for innovation<br>• Invest $5B in sustainable products<br>• Create services BU | • Implement "digital twin" for manufacturing<br>• Reengineer supply chain<br>• Implement "pricing for value" program | • Divest low-margin businesses X & Y<br>• Acquire high-growth global markets: India and ME | • Strengthen functional competencies<br>• Install global operating model<br>• Revamp performance management |
| **How** will we know we're successful? *(measures)* | • 2x market growth<br>• 10% top-line growth in services | • -20% cost of quality, -50% supply chain costs<br>• +20% revenue on existing products | • -15% growth in target markets<br>• Top-quartile EBITDA multiple | • 95%+ top talent retention<br>• Top-quartile performance culture survey |
| **What** will we stop doing to free capacity? *(resource allocation)* | • No subscale M&A in non-strategic target areas<br>• Don't build-out quality beyond what is valued by the customer<br>• Shut down network of fragmented "skunk works" units<br>• No pushing quality errors down the line to meet schedule<br>• No "one of a kind" innovation (all happens in product families)<br>• No product investments without services strategies | | | |
| **Why** will this matter for our stakeholders? *(stakeholder impact)* | Employees: More opportunities, better enablement, and increased profit sharing<br>Customers: From "a to b" faster, safer, reliably, & responsibly<br>Shareholders: Top-quartile returns vs. Dow Jones average<br>Society: Connect the world more sustainably | | | |

## Reflection Exercise 1: Direction Setting

| | |
|---|---|
| **Where** are we headed? *(reframe the game vision)* | |
| **How** will we make it happen? *(big moves)* | |
| **What** actions will we take? *(initiatives)* | |
| **How** will we know we're successful? *(measures)* | |
| **What** will we stop doing to free capacity? *(resource allocation)* | |
| **Why** will this matter for our stakeholders? *(stakeholder impact)* | Employees:<br><br>Customers:<br><br>Shareholders:<br><br>Society: |

# Reflection Exercise 2: Culture Change

## WHY WE CHOSE THIS REFLECTION EXERCISE

Albert Einstein is said to have had a poster in his office that declared, "Not everything that counts can be counted." In business, culture is a prime example of this. Just because culture isn't readily quantifiable doesn't mean it can't be managed with rigor and discipline. This exercise will help you do so.

## HOW IT SHOULD BE USED

This exercise first asks you a series of questions to help you get to the root cause that's keeping you from unlocking better business performance (what is the "from/to"?). It then asks you to specify a short list of actions that will address your core cultural issue—leveraging the four areas that cognitive and behavioral sciences have shown to have the maximum impact on shifting mindsets and behaviors.

As you reflect, consider whether you have:

- Focused on the **thematic culture shift** most needed to execute your strategy. As a litmus test, ask yourself: *If our people lived in the "to" state, would we materially accelerate progress and achieve more impact?*

- Identified a short list of **observable behaviors** that illustrate the "from" state in a way people would recognize and concretely lays out what the alternative "to" state actions would look like.

- Defined the **mindset unlock** that could cause the needed behavior change. This requires first naming a reasonable, relatable "from" mindset, then reframing an alternative "to" mindset that will inspire the new behaviors.

- Planned how to influence the desired behavior shift. It is crucial to pull all the **influence levers**—but at the same time, you should avoid a laundry list of new to-dos. Look for ways to do the things that happen today (e.g., annual planning processes, performance reviews, onboarding new hires, etc.) differently, versus adding a number of net new initiatives to the slate.

# Reflection Exercise 2: Culture Change (example)

## A. CULTURE SHIFT: *What is one key shift you will focus on?*

| Thematic Culture Shift | From<br>**TRADITIONAL** | → | To<br>**INNOVATIVE** |
|---|---|---|---|
| Observable Behaviors | - Move slowly and only after careful analysis<br>- Avoid failure to every extent possible<br>- Spend majority of time on written plans, updates, and documentation<br>- Innovate only if given permission | → | - Rapidly iterate and "test & learn" to improve solutions<br>- Allow for controlled failure to learn and improve<br>- Spend majority of time in ideation and prototyping<br>- Innovate continuously as part of standard work |
| Mindset Unlock | **Our job is to protect our legacy** | → | **Our job is to shape our industry** |

## B. INFLUENCE MODEL: *How will you influence this desired shift?*

### Role Modeling
*"I see superiors, peers, and subordinates behaving in the new way."*

- Personally model desired approach to failure by openly admitting when a mistake has been made & celebrating failure for the right reasons
- Begin meetings by spotlighting new ideas from employees or learnings from pre- or postmortem sessions

### Storytelling
*"I know what is expected of me— I agree with it, and it is meaningful."*

- Launch cascading series of two-way dialogues where leaders explain needed shift, share personal "failure-as-a-win story," & discuss how team will evolve
- Embed language markers ("success is the far side of failure") into all ongoing communications

### Skill and Confidence Building
*"I have the skills, competencies, and opportunities to behave in the new way."*

- Create "prototyping playbook" and teach managers what "test & learn" looks like in practice (including having them identify specific ways to apply)
- Launch an annual hackathon that includes learning-by-doing apprenticeship on rapid ideation

### Reinforcing Mechanisms
*"Structures, processes, incentives, and systems reinforce the change."*

- Redesign performance management to celebrate smart risk-taking & learning from failure (vs. "just" success)
- Radically simplify quarterly business reports and monthly operating reviews—less time on documents, more time in dialogue/doing

# Reflection Exercise 2: Culture Change

| A. CULTURE SHIFT: *What is one key shift you will focus on?* | | |
|---|---|---|
| Thematic Culture Shift | From → | To |
| Observable Behaviors | → | |
| Mindset Unlock | → | |

| B. INFLUENCE MODEL: *How will you influence this desired shift?* | |
|---|---|
| **Role Modeling** *"I see superiors, peers, and subordinates behaving in the new way."* | **Storytelling** *"I know what is expected of me— I agree with it, and it is meaningful."* |
| **Skill and Confidence Building** *"I have the skills, competencies, and opportunities to behave in the new way."* | **Reinforcing Mechanisms** *"Structures, processes, incentives, and systems reinforce the change."* |

## Reflection Exercise 3: Team Performance

### WHY WE CHOSE THIS REFLECTION EXERCISE

Franklin D. Roosevelt, the thirty-second president of the United States, once said, "I'm not the smartest fellow in the world, but I can sure pick smart colleagues." Similarly, the best CEOs are very savvy and selective about who sits on their team. This reflection helps ensure you have the right people in the right roles.

### HOW IT SHOULD BE USED

In this exercise, you will prioritize roles by their importance to your strategy, then specify exactly what you need those roles to deliver. From there, you're asked to analyze to what extent the people in those roles today have the right capability and mindset for the job. The last step is to craft a person-by-person game plan to maximize the probability of success.

As you reflect, consider whether you have:

- Defined which **roles** are most critical to achieving your strategy. Some of those roles may be on your top team; others may be one or more layers down in the organization. Some may not even exist within the organization today.

- Clearly articulated the top three to five **outcomes** you need each leader to deliver. These should be specific results needed (actions and/or outcomes) with deadlines—not generic job descriptions.

- Reflected holistically upon the hard and soft **capabilities** required to deliver the results you need. It is important to take a forward-looking lens, rather than relying on what it took for people in the role to be successful in the past.

- Examined deeply the **mindset** of each leader, including their level of commitment to both *what* is expected of them and *how* they're expected to do it (e.g., playing team ball, taking accountability, showing resilience).

- Distilled the **implications** for your role, such as putting in place the conditions for your team members to be successful (e.g., coaching, role modeling, incentives, skill building). As you do so, guard against any biases or patterns that might steer you in the wrong direction when assessing leaders.

## Reflection Exercise 3: Team Performance (example)

### A. ROLES AND MISSIONS
*What are the top five roles most critical to achieving your strategy?*
*What are the most important missions for this role to deliver on?*

**CTO (Tony S):** Run successful digital transformation (20% productivity gain in Wave 1 functions); implement target operating model (10% efficiencies from reduced fragmentation of tech capabilities); launch new AI platform by Q3

**CCO (Meg R):** Grow prioritized key accounts by 15% (+5 pts vs. overall growth); build system to ensure client input incorporated in product development plans (60% of Tier 1 product dev plans get input by Q2, 100% by Q4); improve NPS scores to >70%

**CHRO (Sean F):** Build talent acquisition engine that halves time-to-hire for priority roles by Q2; drive adoption of needed culture shifts (70% of leaders scored as "great" role models in EOY survey); deliver on time, on budget HRIS

**CFO (Nancy L):** Execute investor road show to build confidence in new strategy (next 100 days); build credible budget for next year that enables operating plan while meeting near-term cash flow expectations; lead diligence & deal for target

**Product X leader (Frank N; sits 1-2 levels below CEO):** Successfully lead product X launch—>$70M in revenue in first 18 months (with runway to $200M by year 3); maintain quality through scaling; improve working relationship with marketing team

### B. PLOT YOUR LEADERS
*Where would you plot the leaders currently in each role on this matrix?*

### C. IMPLICATIONS
*How will you get leaders where they need to be?*

**CFO (Nancy L):** Needs improvement in handling investor expectations due to limited IR engagement. Will mentor her to own a resilient, long-term narrative. Need to see real progress over next three months.

**CHRO (Sean F):** Passionate about people/org but not expert in HR best practices (came from business role). Set him up to attend industry roundtables and network with other CHROs. We'll have recurring 1:1s to track progress over next six months.

## Reflection Exercise 3: Team Performance

**A. ROLES AND MISSIONS**
*What are the top five roles most critical to achieving your strategy?*
*What are the most important missions for this role to deliver on?*

**B. PLOT YOUR LEADERS**
*Where would you plot the leaders currently in each role on this matrix?*

**C. IMPLICATIONS**
*How will you get leaders where they need to be?*

Capability (HIGH / LOW) vs. Mindset (LOW / HIGH)

# Reflection Exercise 4: Board Effectiveness

### WHY WE CHOSE THIS REFLECTION EXERCISE

Mother Teresa proclaimed, "I can do things you cannot. You can do things I cannot. Together we can do great things." In that spirit, the most effective senior leaders do everything they can to help their boards help the business. This exercise helps you lay out essential parts of a plan to do so.

### HOW IT SHOULD BE USED

First, this exercise asks you to map out the capabilities you would like to have on the board and assess whether those are present today. Next, you will gauge the strength of your relationships with each member. By doing this, you can identify opportunities to improve how you work with board members, engage their expertise, and encourage changes in the board's composition—in partnership with the board chairperson (or lead independent director).

As you reflect, consider whether you have:

- Prioritized the most essential **capabilities** needed on the board based on your strategic direction and the evergreen considerations that are so important for good governance.

- Assessed the **strength** of each director's expertise against those capabilities and the strength of your personal relationship with the board. Both are foundational to being able to successfully enable the board to help the business.
- Identified specific **actions** you will take as a result, either directly or through discussion with your chairperson.

## Reflection Exercise 4: Board Effectiveness (example)

*How strong are the capabilities of each director on your board?*

| Capability | RW | MP | NM | CW | MB | JD | CC | VK | Notes |
|---|---|---|---|---|---|---|---|---|---|
| **M&A** | Deep | Deep | Distinctive | Distinctive | Some | Limited | Deep | Deep | Wealth of expertise on board |
| **Turnarounds** | Limited | Distinctive | Deep | Some | Some | Limited | Distinctive | Some | Should tap into more fully |
| **Cyber** | Some | Some | Some | Some | Deep | Some | Some | Deep | Potential blind spot; need to fix |
| **India** | Distinctive | Some | Some | Some | Limited | Some | Some | Some | Critical to growth strategy |
| **Regulatory** | Distinctive | Deep | Some | Deep | Some | Distinctive | Deep | Deep | Can do more to leverage |
| **Strength of Relationship** | MED | MED | HIGH | LOW | HIGH | LOW | MED | MED | Weakest w/ our newest directors |

| | |
|---|---|
| What **actions will you take** to strengthen relationships? | ▪ CW: Get quarterly dinners (values social connection)—ask for feedback, engage on M&A<br>▪ JD: Consult on regulatory issues via ad hoc calls (prefers targeted, content-based) |
| What **other actions** might you consider (education, transparency, board meeting norms)? | ▪ Test with chair—can we explore profiles with India expertise/networks when NM term ends?<br>▪ Shift agenda to start & end with exec session—share transparently, get feedback |

**Legend:**
- ● Truly distinctive, best-in-class thought leader
- ◕ Deep expert and trusted advisor
- ◐ Some expertise; okay if some minor gaps
- ◔ Limited expertise
- ○ No relevant expertise

**Reflection Exercises** | **129**

## Reflection Exercise 4: Board Effectiveness

*How strong are the capabilities of each director on your board?*

| Capability | BOARD DIRECTORS → | Notes |
|---|---|---|
| | ● ● ● ● ● ● ● | |
| | ● ● ● ● ● ● ● | |
| | ● ● ● ● ● ● ● | |
| | ● ● ● ● ● ● ● | |
| | ● ● ● ● ● ● ● | |
| **Strength of Relationship** | | |

| What **actions will you take** to strengthen relationships? | |
|---|---|

| What **other actions** might you consider (education, transparency, board meeting norms)? | |
|---|---|

● Truly distinctive, best-in-class thought leader
◐ Deep expert and trusted advisor
◑ Some expertise; okay if some minor gaps
◓ Limited expertise
○ No relevant expertise

## Reflection Exercise 5: Stakeholder Engagement

**WHY WE CHOSE THIS REFLECTION EXERCISE**

Most people ascribe to the Golden Rule—that is, "Treat others the way you want to be treated." When it comes to stakeholder management, however, a different approach can have a higher impact: "Treat others the way *they* want to be treated." We refer to this as the Platinum Rule. This reflection prompts you to consider the world from the perspective of your most important stakeholders in ways that ideally will lead to more win–win outcomes.

**HOW IT SHOULD BE USED**

The exercise begins by triaging which stakeholders are most important for you to attend to and prompts a synthesis of the needs they have (their "why"). It then evaluates how those needs intersect with you and your organization's goals (your "why") and explores ways to optimize outcomes and foster even stronger, more effective relationships.

As you reflect, consider whether you have:

- Accurately assessed your **relationship strength** with the stakeholders most critical to your strategy (e.g., a specific regulator, a key supplier, an activist investor).

- Captured the essence of your stakeholders' underlying needs (**their "why"**). Figure out what they are solving for, both organizationally and individually.

- Clearly articulated **your own "why"**—what you are hoping to achieve relative to this stakeholder. It's helpful to clarify both a "highest hope" and "minimum requirement."

- Thought creatively about **how these "whys" intersect**. This can take unexpected forms (for example, listening deeply to a seemingly antagonistic stakeholder can surface new ideas for you and make them more friendly).

- Defined how you will **engage differently or better** having methodically thought through all of the above. Seeking counsel from your closest colleagues and counselors can help push your thinking here.

# Reflection Exercise 5: Stakeholder Engagement (example)

## A. PRIORITIZATION
*Who are the most important stakeholders who impact your business?*

| Stakeholder Name | Relationship Strength |
|---|---|
| Major Customer 1 | Very Strong |
| Major Customer 2 | Strong |
| Media Outlet 1 | Amicable |
| US Attorney General for Antitrust | Weak |
| EU Competition Commission Director | Weak |
| Merger Target | Very Strong |
| JV Partner | Very Strong |
| Analyst at Bank A (opinion maker) | Amicable |
| Key Investor 1 | Weak |
| Key Investor 2 | Strong |

Legend:
- ● Very Strong
- ◕ Strong
- ◑ Amicable
- ◔ Weak
- ○ No Relationship or Combative

## B. ACTION PLAN
*Use the following as a template to evaluate one stakeholder from your list, then repeat with others.*

Stakeholder name: **Major Customer 1 — CFO (Tina J, new in role)**

| Their Needs *(their "why")* | Our Needs *(our "why")* |
|---|---|
| Deliver sustainable growth, avoid "surprises" in results, establish credibility as new CFO | High-potential account—Fortune 500 company, we only serve with one product, target 20% YoY |
| *How do **our "whys"** intersect? (common interests)* | *Knowing this, how can you **interact differently?*** |
| Product X's AI/analytics can predict risks relevant to client (financial, ops)—can tailor to their subsector | Bring our CFO to next mtg to explain value prop in a peer-to-peer counseling conversation (vs. "salesy") |

## Reflection Exercise 5: Stakeholder Engagement

### A. PRIORITIZATION
*Who are the most important stakeholders who impact your business?*

| Stakeholder Name | Relationship Strength |
|---|---|
| | |
| | |
| | |
| | |
| | |
| | |
| | |
| | |
| | |
| | |

- ● Very Strong
- ◐ Strong
- ◑ Amicable
- ◕ Weak
- ○ No Relationship or Combative

### B. ACTION PLAN
*Use the following as a template to evaluate one stakeholder from your list, then repeat with others.*

Stakeholder name:

| Their Needs *(their "why")* | Our Needs *(our "why")* |
|---|---|
| | |
| *How do **our "whys"** intersect? (common interests)* | *Knowing this, how can you **interact differently**?* |
| | |

# Reflection Exercise 6: Personal Leadership Effectiveness

## WHY WE CHOSE THIS REFLECTION EXERCISE

The notion of "situational leadership" was introduced almost fifty years ago by Dr. Paul Hersey, author of *The Situational Leader*, and Kenneth Blanchard, author of *The One Minute Manager*. The thesis is that if leaders can adapt their style to the situation—while maintaining their authenticity—they'll be able to achieve superior results. This reflection helps you ensure you are most effectively walking that line.

## HOW IT SHOULD BE USED

This exercise asks you to take a step back from the day-to-day to reflect more deeply on who you are as a leader and whether that's what the organization needs. It's most helpful when the reflection is done with trusted counselors who will both call out tough truths and celebrate hidden strengths. You can also use it to coach your potential successors to make sure they develop the necessary qualities for the CEO role.

As you reflect, consider whether you have:

- Thought fully about what **your organization needs** from its CEO. Link the desired leadership qualities to your strategy—it shouldn't be a generic "good leader" list. Find out what multiple stakeholders (e.g., top team, employees, board, shareholders, customers, regulators) expect of you.

- Candidly "held up the mirror" on how **you are currently perceived** as a leader. Be objective and listen to both supporters and critics, asking if you bring the necessary knowledge, skills, experiences, relationships, and leadership.

- Identified the **implications for your leadership style**—how you can build on strengths and address gaps. This could include a wide range of actions (experimenting with new behaviors, getting help from others, putting new structures in place, etc.).

## Reflection Exercise 6:
## Personal Leadership Effectiveness (example)

### A. IDEAL LEADERSHIP CHARACTERISTICS
*What does your organization need from its CEO in the next ~12 months to achieve the company's objectives?*

- **Provocative Visionary** – Bold thinker, not anchored to current state; agitates for change; inspires others to think big; introduces new ideas
- **Disciplined Executor** – Sees ideas through; relentlessly focused on driving results; avoids fragmentation & ruthlessly prioritizes
- **Convener & Connector** – Bridges across BUs and regions; uses healthy tension to create buy-in (NOT discord); builds coalition of leaders ready to drive change
- **Talent Developer** – Builds capabilities in others (coaching, feedback, apprenticeship); builds high-performing team; enables others to shine

### B. PERCEPTIONS OF YOUR LEADERSHIP
*Given what the CEO role will demand of you . . .*

| What would **supporters** call out as reasons you will excel? | What would **critics** call out as reasons you will struggle? |
|---|---|
| - Big thinker, good at bringing in ideas from outside our org | - Cycles through ideas vs. sticks to a few good ones; not execution-oriented |
| - Effective challenger, pushes colleagues to think critically | - Can sometimes make others feel alienated when challenging their ideas |
| - Processes input very quickly & decisively | - My ideas become "law," especially when I speak first—others don't engage |
| - Caring leader, strong relationships with C-suite & many in my old BU | - Unknown to half the org (other BUs) |

### C. IMPLICATIONS
*What are the implications of the above? What steps can you take to close the gaps and continue to grow as a leader?*

- Consider appointing a "Chief Transformation Officer" to help drive execution discipline and follow-through on my bold strategy
- Ensure I have a "naysayer"/"truth teller" in my informal network to ensure I'm not just hearing what I want to hear, but what I need to hear
- Show self-awareness and disarm cynics by naming negative perceptions & acknowledging tendencies, sharing mitigation plans, & asking for help
- Spend disproportionate time up front helping the other BUs get to know me

## Reflection Exercise 6:
## Personal Leadership Effectiveness

**A. IDEAL LEADERSHIP CHARACTERISTICS**
*What does your organization need from its CEO in the next ~12 months to achieve the company's objectives?*

**B. PERCEPTIONS OF YOUR LEADERSHIP**
*Given what the CEO role will demand of you . . .*

| *What would **supporters** call out as reasons you will excel?* | *What would **critics** call out as reasons you will struggle?* |
| --- | --- |
| | |

**C. IMPLICATIONS**
*What are the implications of the above? What steps can you take to close the gaps and continue to grow as a leader?*

APPENDIX B:
# CEO Biographies

Although four of us took the lead in writing this book, the author list could rightfully extend to all the exceptional CEOs we interviewed along the way. Their stories are such that a book could be dedicated to each. In the following pages we include biographies of all those CEOs we've quoted in the text who are also on our top 200 list.

# LILACH ASHER-TOPILSKY
**ISRAEL DISCOUNT BANK**

Revenue: $4B
Market cap: $8B
Employees: 9k in 3 countries

**Career Highlights**

Israel Discount Bank: Chairperson & CEO (2014–2019)
Fimi Opportunity Funds: Senior Partner (2019–present)

**Other Roles and Boards**

- Chair of Kamada (NASDAQ), Rimoni Industries (TASE), Amal and Beyond, Elyakim Ben Ari, and Marom Dolphin
- On the boards of Amiad Water Systems (TASE), Ashot Ashkelon (TASE), and Tel-Aviv University

**CEO Impact**

- Changed the trajectory of Israel's third-largest bank, raising net income threefold, slashing its cost / income ratio by almost 20%, and reestablishing a productive relationship with the unions.

**Fast Facts**

- Received the *Jerusalem Post* award for leaving her mark on the banking sector, 2019
- Became youngest CEO of an Israeli bank

# OLIVER BÄTE
**ALLIANZ SE**

Revenue: $165B
Market cap: $119B
Employees: 160k in 70+ countries

**Career Highlights**

Allianz SE: CEO (2015–present)
McKinsey & Company: Director of the European Insurance and Asset Management Sector

**Other Roles and Boards**

- On the boards of the Pan-European Insurance Forum (PEIF), Institute of International Finance (IFF), and Geneva Association
- On the advisory boards of the Council on Foreign Relations, Munich Security Conference, and Monetary Authority of Singapore (MAS)

**CEO Impact**

- Transformed Allianz into a global leader in insurance and asset management through a series of consistent strategic acquisitions and digitalization investments, increasing market cap more than 50% during his tenure. Put sustainability at the forefront of Allianz's agenda, committing to tackling global warming and reducing the carbon emissions of investment portfolios to net-zero by 2050 and helping set up the Net-Zero Asset Owner Alliance.

**Fast Facts**

- Named on *Harvard Business Review*'s The Best-Performing CEOs in the World, 2019
- Received the John J McCloy Award from the American Council on Germany
- Member of the World Economic Forum Stewardship Board of the Initiative on Shaping the Future of Financial and Monetary Systems, 2017

## GAIL BOUDREAUX
### ELEVANCE HEALTH
### (FORMERLY ANTHEM, INC.)

Revenue: $170B
Market cap: $86B
Employees: 100k globally

**Career Highlights**

Elevance Health: President & CEO (2017–present)
UnitedHealthcare: CEO (2011–2014)

**Other Roles and Boards**

- Chair of The Business Council
- Trustee of the Field Museum of Natural History
- On the boards of Target, Blue Cross Blue Shield Association, and American Health Insurance Plans

**CEO Impact**

- Led several strategic acquisitions for Elevance Health to expand market presence and enter new verticals, with revenue almost doubling during her tenure. Focused on talent development through mentoring and promoting women leaders, resulting in a workforce that is 75%+ women and executive team that is 60%+ women.
- Her leadership transformed Elevance Health into a high-performing execution company that has consistently delivered results since.

**Fast Facts**

- Named on *Forbes'* World's Most Powerful Women, 2024, and 50 over 50: Innovation, 2023
- Named one of the 100 Most Influential People in Healthcare by *Modern Healthcare*, 2024
- Awarded NCAA's highest honor for athletes, the Theodore Roosevelt Award, 2022
- Recipient of the Billie Jean King Leadership Award, 2018

## PETER BRABECK-LETMATHE
### NESTLÉ

Revenue: $111B
Market cap: $212B
Employees: 270k in 100+ countries

**Career Highlights**

Nestlé: Chair Emeritus (2017–present); Chair (2005–2017); CEO (1997–2008)
Formula 1 Group: Chair (2012–2016)

**Other Roles and Boards**

- Chair of Biologique Recherche, GESDA (Geneva Science & Diplomacy Anticipator), SES-imagotag Advisory Board, and Business Policy International Advisory Board of San Telmo Business School
- Vice-Chair of the World Economic Forum Board of Trustees

**CEO Impact**

- Grew the already sizeable Swiss food company by focusing on cost cutting, innovation, and speed of decision-making, while also acquiring the pet food company Ralston Purina. Refreshed at least 20% of products every year, shifting the company's focus to nutrition, health, and wellness, while almost tripling market cap.

**Fast Facts**

- Founder and chairman of 2030 Water Resources Group, a public-private partnership incorporated as part of the World Bank
- Awarded La Orden Francisco de Miranda, Republic of Venezuela
- Awarded the Austrian Cross of Honor for service to the Republic of Austria
- Awarded the Mexican Order of the Aztec Eagle

## GREG CASE
### AON

Revenue: $13B
Market cap: $78B
Employees: 60k in 120 countries

**Career Highlights**

Aon: CEO (2005–present)

**Other Roles and Boards**

- On the boards of Ann & Robert H. Lurie Children's Hospital, Field Museum of Natural History, St. John's University School of Risk Management, and Intersect Illinois

**CEO Impact**

- Reorganized the global risk mitigator's portfolio through a series of bold M&A deals and divestitures, while undertaking a major cultural and operational transformation that has helped the Irish-domiciled firm double revenue and increase market cap tenfold over his tenure so far. He installed a notion of resilience as a company-building capability, which can drive opportunity in times of volatility.

**Fast Facts**

- Appeared five times in *HBR*'s Top 100 CEOs
- Received the Committee for Economic Development's Owen B. Butler Education Excellence Award, 2018
- Has received multiple awards for his role as an ally and advocate for inclusion and diversity

## KEN CHENAULT
**AMERICAN EXPRESS**

Revenue: $61B
Market cap: $209B
Employees: 75k in 35+ countries

**Career Highlights**

American Express: Chairman & CEO (2001–2018)

**Other Roles and Boards**

- Chair, General Catalyst Partners and Bilt
- Co-Chair of Concordance's First Chance campaign to end the cycle of reincarceration
- On the boards of Airbnb, Chief, Guild Education, the Harvard Corporation, and numerous nonprofit organizations
- Co-Founder of OneTen, a coalition of leading executives that aims to upskill, hire, and advance one million Black Americans over the next ten years into family-sustaining jobs with opportunities for advancement

**CEO Impact**

- Expanded American Express' core business beyond T&E spending to serve the needs of its members across spending categories. Under his leadership, the company introduced and built one of the world's largest customer loyalty programs (Membership Rewards) and earned global recognition as a leader in customer service, while doubling revenue and growing net income more than fivefold.

**Fast Facts**

- Named in *Barron's* World's Best CEOs list multiple times
- Named in *Forbes'* inaugural BLK50 list in 2024
- Named one of the 100 Most Influential People in the World by *Time*, 2021
- Honored by *HistoryMakers* in 2018, celebrating his extraordinary life and career
- Listed as one of fifty "living pioneers" in the African American community by *Ebony*

# LARRY CULP
## GENERAL ELECTRIC

Revenue: $24B
Market cap: $166B
Employees: 63k in 50 countries

**Career Highlights**

**General Electric:** Chair & CEO (2018–2024); CEO, GE Aerospace (2022–present); Chairman, GE Aerospace (2024–present)
**Danaher:** CEO (2001–2014)

**Other Roles and Boards**

- On the boards of Washington College and Wake Forest University

**CEO Impact**

- Scaled the concept of lean management to all aspects of the business at Danaher, improving efficiencies through a high-performance culture while freeing up capital to acquire high-growth businesses. Increased both revenue and market cap fivefold. As Chairman and CEO of GE, Larry Culp led the company's financial and operational transformation, reducing debt by over $100B.

**Fast Facts**

- Named one of *Barron's* Top 25 CEOs in the world four times since 2020
- Ranked as one of the top CEOs in annual Institutional Investor surveys, and named one of the Top 50 CEOs in the world by *Harvard Business Review*
- Previously a Senior Lecturer at Harvard Business School

# SANDY CUTLER
## EATON CORPORATION

Revenue: $23B
Market cap: $132B
Employees: 92k in 60+ countries

### Career Highlights

Eaton Corporation: Chair & CEO (2000–2016)

### Other Roles and Boards

- Co-Lead Director of DowDuPont
- Honorary Trustee for Life of the Cleveland Orchestra
- On the boards of KeyCorp, United Way of Greater Cleveland, and the Musical Arts Association

### CEO Impact

- Diversified the US auto-parts maker into a power management company to stimulate growth, while promoting a culture of innovation, impact, and integrity. Grew revenue fivefold and market cap almost sevenfold.

### Fast Facts

- Appeared twice in *HBR*'s Top 100 CEOs
- Opened a high-end French-American restaurant with his wife and son
- Established the Cutler Center for Men at University Hospitals with his wife to provide physical, emotional, and mental health services
- Established the Sarah S. and Alexander M. Cutler Center for Student Success and Academic Achievement to help first-generation students at Albion College

# RICHARD DAVIS

## U.S. BANCORP

Revenue: $28B
Market cap: $75B
Employees: 70k+ in 13 countries

### Career Highlights

U.S. Bancorp: Chairman & CEO (2006–2017)
Make-A-Wish Foundation: President & CEO (2019–2022)

### Other Roles and Boards

- Lead Director of Dow Inc.
- On the boards of Mastercard, Mayo Clinic Board of Trustees, and Wells Fargo

### CEO Impact

- Put customers and employees at the heart of a ten-year vision to expand the US bank's operations, while actively serving the local community. Grew net income by 30% and stock price by more than 60%.

### Fast Facts

- Granted the US President's Lifetime Achievement Award, 2015
- U.S. Bancorp was awarded the Freedom Award under his leadership, the highest recognition given by the US Department of Defense to employers for their support of employees who serve in the National Guard and Reserve, 2013
- Named Banker of the Year by *American Banker*, 2010

# MICHAEL DELL
**DELL TECHNOLOGIES**

Revenue: $102B
Market cap: $81B
Employees: 133k in 180+ countries

### Career Highlights
**Dell Technologies:** Founder & CEO (1984–2004, 2007–present); Chair (2016–present)

### Other Roles and Boards
- Founder of DFO Management and the Michael & Susan Dell Foundation
- Chair of the BDT & MSD Partners Advisory Board
- Honorary member of the Foundation Board of the World Economic Forum
- Member of the International Business Council Executive Committee, Technology CEO Council, and The Business Roundtable
- On the advisory board of Tsinghua University's School of Economics and Management and governing board of the Indian School of Business

### CEO Impact
- Founded Dell Technologies in 1984 at the age of 19 and went on to pioneer the direct-to-consumer PC segment. Made a series of bold moves and acquisitions, including conducting the largest tech acquisition at the time, of EMC in 2016, valued at $67B. Positioned the company as a global leader in enterprise IT and cloud computing, providing tech infrastructure for 99% of Fortune 500 companies.

### Fast Facts
- Author of two books, *Direct from Dell* and *Play Nice But Win*
- Named as the United Nations Foundation's Global Advocate for Entrepreneurship, 2014
- Awarded the Franklin Institute's Bower Award for Business Leadership, 2013
- Received the Golden Plate Award of the American Academy of Achievement, 1998
- Became the youngest CEO ever to earn a ranking on the Fortune 500 in 1992 and has been listed on the Fortune 500 nearly every year since

# JAMIE DIMON
## JPMORGAN CHASE

Revenue: $158B
Market cap: $675B
Employees: 300k+ in 100+ countries

**Career Highlights**

JPMorgan Chase: CEO (2006–present); Chair (2007–present)
Bank One: CEO & Chair (2000–2004)

**Other Roles and Boards**

- On the boards of Business Roundtable, Bank Policy Institute, Catalyst, and Partnership for New York City
- Member of Business Council, Financial Services Forum, and Council on Foreign Relations

**CEO Impact**

- Built resilience into America's largest bank ahead of the 2008 financial crisis, enabling it to withstand the shock. Helped shore up the nation's banking system, while becoming a leading voice in the business world known for his transparency. The only surviving major bank CEO from the financial crisis, he has more than quadrupled JPMC's market cap, making it the most valuable bank in the world.

**Fast Facts**

- Recognized by *Fortune* as one of the 5 Most Powerful People in Business, 2024
- Named multiple times in *Time*'s 100 Most Influential People list
- Voted *Fortune*'s Most Admired Fortune 500 CEO, 2019 & 2020

# LARRY FINK
## BLACKROCK, INC.

Revenue: $18B
Market cap: $159B
Employees: 20k in 35 countries

### Career Highlights

BlackRock: Chairman & CEO
(1988-present, cofounded the company)

### Other Roles and Boards

- First Boston Corporation: Managing Director (1976–1988)
- Co-Chair of the NYU Langone Medical Center Board of Trustees; on the boards of the World Economic Forum, Museum of Modern Art, and International Rescue Committee
- On the advisory boards of the Tsinghua University School of Economics and Management in Beijing and the Partnership for New York City

### CEO Impact

- As a founder-CEO, built BlackRock's global footprint, growing it to more than 75 offices in more than 35 countries, and generating an annualized total return of 21% for shareholders since the company's IPO in 1999 (well in excess of S&P 500 return of 8%). Today, BlackRock stands as the world's largest asset manager, with more than $11T AUM (as of FY24).

### Fast Facts

- Named one of the World's Greatest Leaders by *Fortune*, and *Barron's* named him one of the World's Best CEOs for 15 consecutive years
- Named to *Fortune*'s 100 Most Powerful People in Business, 2024
- Earned multiple awards and honors, including the Charles Schwab Financial Innovation Award in 2019, UCLA Medal in 2016, Americas Society Gold Medal in 2015, and Woodrow Wilson Award in 2010

## MICHAEL FISHER
### CINCINNATI CHILDREN'S HOSPITAL MEDICAL CENTER

Revenue: $3B
Market cap: N/A
Employees: 20k in Cincinnati

**Career Highlights**

Cincinnati Children's Hospital Medical Center: President & CEO (2010–2021)
Cincinnati Chamber of Commerce: CEO (2001–2005)

**CEO Impact**

- Significantly upgraded the Cincinnati Children's Hospital's capabilities as a premier academic medical research center, while improving access and experience for patients and families, and substantially increasing partnerships to address social determinants of health. Roughly tripled endowment growth, doubled revenue, and doubled patient care capacity.

**Fast Facts**

- Named *Cincinnati Business Courier*'s Health Care Heroes Lifetime Achievement Award winner, 2022
- Named in *Modern Healthcare*'s 100 Most Influential People in Healthcare, 2017
- Cincinnati Children's ranked in the top five for ten consecutive years in *U.S. News & World Report*'s Best Children's Hospitals list

# KEN FRAZIER
## MERCK

**Revenue:** $60B
**Market cap:** $252B
**Employees:** 72k in 70+ countries

### Career Highlights
Merck: Chair (2011–2022); CEO (2011–2021)

### Other Roles and Boards
- Co-Founder and Co-Chair of OneTen
- Chair of Health Assurance Initiatives at General Catalyst
- Co-Chair of Legal Services Corporation's Leaders Council
- On the boards of Eikon Therapeutics, Paradigm, National Constitution Center, Cornerstone Christian Academy, and Weill Cornell Medicine
- Fellow of Harvard College

### CEO Impact
- Substantially increased investment in research and refocused the organization on the launch and growth of key products that provide far-reaching benefits to society. Delivered innovative lifesaving medicines and vaccines, as well as long-term and sustainable value to multiple stakeholders. Merck stock price more than doubled and market cap increased almost 70% during his tenure.

### Fast Facts
- Received an American Bar Association Presidential Citation, 2024; and the Harvard Law School Association Award, 2018
- Named CEO of the Year by *Chief Executive Magazine*, 2021; one of *Time*'s 100 Most Influential People, 2018 & 2021; and one of *Fortune*'s World's Greatest Leaders, 2018
- Honored at Brennan Center for Justice's Legacy Awards, 2021
- First recipient of *Forbes* Lifetime Achievement Award for Healthcare, 2019
- Established the Frazier Family Coalition for stroke education and prevention focused on supporting African American communities in North Philadelphia

# ADENA FRIEDMAN
## NASDAQ

Revenue: $6B
Market cap: $44B
Employees: 9k in 38 countries

**Career Highlights**

**Carlyle Group:** CFO & Managing Director (2011–2014)
**Nasdaq:** CEO (2017–present); Chair (2023–present)

**Other Roles and Boards**

- Chair of the Business Round Table Technology Committee
- On the boards of Federal Reserve Bank of New York and Vanderbilt University

**CEO Impact**

- Spearheaded Nasdaq's evolution into the leading global technology provider to the global financial system. Scaled company's Financial Technology platform, now serving 3,800 clients worldwide. Grew net revenue over 90% and quadrupled market cap over her tenure so far.

**Fast Facts**

- Named one of *Forbes'* World's 100 Most Powerful Women and *Fortune's* Most Powerful Women multiple times since 2020
- Named one of *Barron's* Top 30 CEOs, 2021
- First woman CEO to lead a global stock exchange

# BILL GEORGE
## MEDTRONIC

**Revenue:** $32B
**Market cap:** $102B
**Employees:** 95k in 29 countries

### Career Highlights

**Medtronic:** Chairman (1996–2002); CEO (1991–2001)
**Harvard Business School:** Executive Fellow (2022–present)

### Other Roles and Boards

- Author of best-selling book, *True North: Discover Your Authentic Leadership* (2007)
- Emeritus Public Trustee of the Mayo Clinic
- Lifetime Director of the Guthrie Theater
- On the board of YMCA of the North

### CEO Impact

- Diversified the US medical device company's portfolio through a bold M&A strategy that grew company revenue fivefold and increased market cap more than twelvefold. Measured success by how many seconds it took until someone was helped by a Medtronic product, which decreased from one hundred to seven seconds by the end of his tenure.

### Fast Facts

- Frequently shares his thoughts on trending topics with various media outlets, including *Fortune*, *Forbes*, and the *Harvard Business School Working Knowledge* publication, among others
- Received the Bower Award for Business Leadership from the Franklin Institute, 2014
- Received the Arthur W. Page Center's Larry Foster Award for Integrity in Public Communication, 2018
- Named one of the 25 Most Influential Business People of the Last 20 Years by PBS & Wharton School of Business, 2002

# JAMES GORMAN
## MORGAN STANLEY

Revenue: $54B
Market cap: $203B
Employees: 80k in 42 countries

### Career Highlights

Morgan Stanley: Chair Emeritus (2025–present); Executive Chairman (2024); Chairman (2012–2023); CEO (2010–2023)

### Other Roles and Boards

- Chair of The Walt Disney Co.
- Chair of the Board of Overseers of the Columbia Business School
- Trustee of Columbia University
- On the board of the Council on Foreign Relations

### CEO Impact

- Reshaped the portfolio of the global financial services firm during his tenure as one of the longest-serving CEOs on Wall Street. Led the firm through recovery from the 2008 financial crisis and onto a decade of growth and profitability. Over his tenure, Morgan Stanley's stock price and market capitalization more than tripled.

### Fast Facts

- Ranked tenth on *FinTech Magazine*'s Top CEOs in Banking, 2024
- Appointed as an Officer of the Order of Australia, 2020
- Received the Whitehead Award from the Museum of American Finance, 2020
- Included in the 50 Most Influential ranking of the *Bloomberg Markets* magazine in 2014 & 2020

# DR. ROBERT GROSSMAN
## NYU LANGONE HEALTH

Revenue: $12B
Market cap: N/A
Employees: 52k in the US

**Career Highlights**

NYU Langone Health: Dean & CEO (2007–present)

**Other Roles and Boards**

- On the board of the Greater New York Hospital Foundation

**CEO Impact**

- Transformed NYU Langone into one of the leading academic medical centers in the US. Applied a data-driven approach to health care with a signature 800-metric dashboard and launched a decade-long infrastructure modernization program that has expanded NYU Langone's footprint. Increased revenue sevenfold during his tenure.

**Fast Facts**

- Elected to the American Academy of Arts and Sciences for excellence and leadership, 2022
- Received the American Society of Neuroradiology Gold Medal for his contributions to the field of neuroradiology, 2021
- Named to *Time*'s inaugural The Healthcare 50 list of the most influential health care leaders who changed the state of health care in America, 2018
- Authored 340 publications and 5 books

# PIYUSH GUPTA
## DBS GROUP

Revenue: $15B
Market cap: $92B
Employees: 40k in 15 countries

**Career Highlights**

DBS Group: CEO (2009–present)

**Other Roles and Boards**

- Chair of Singapore Management University Board of Trustees and the Mandai Park Holdings Board
- Co-Chairman of the BirdLife International Advisory Group
- Vice-Chair of the International Institute of Finance
- Term Trustee of the Singapore Indian Development Association (SINDA)
- On the board of Singapore's National Research Foundation
- Member of Singapore's Advisory Council on the Ethical Use of AI and Data

**CEO Impact**

- Turned around the Singapore bank, now the largest bank in Southeast Asia, by reinvigorating employees and redefining it as a technology company that delivers financial services. Tripled revenue and grew market cap by sevenfold so far during his tenure.

**Fast Facts**

- Awarded the Pravasi Bharatiya Samman Award, the highest honor conferred by the Indian Government on the country's diaspora, 2023
- Awarded Global Indian of the Year by the *Economic Times*, 2021
- Awarded the Public Service Star by the president of Singapore, 2020
- Appeared in *HBR*'s Top 100 CEOs, 2019
- DBS ranked tenth in *HBR*'s Top 20 Business Transformations of the Last Decade, 2019
- DBS named World's Best Bank 2018, 2019, & 2020 by *Global Finance*, *Euromoney*, and *The Banker*

## HERBERT HAINER
### ADIDAS

Revenue: $24B
Market cap: $44B
Employees: 59k in 20+ countries

**Career Highlights**

**Adidas:** Chair & CEO (2001–2016)
**FC Bayern München:** Chairman & President (2019–present)

**CEO Impact**

- Boosted the international footprint of the German sportswear company by investing in brands and R&D, while pushing the organization to deliver on the mission of being the best sports brand. Tripled revenue and increased market cap tenfold.

**Fast Facts**

- Appeared three times in *HBR*'s Top 100 CEOs (once in the top 5)
- Received the Order of Merit of the Federal Republic of Germany, 2008, and the Bavarian Order of Merit, 2011

# REED HASTINGS
## NETFLIX

Revenue: $34B
Market cap: $381B
Employees: 13k in 25+ countries

### Career Highlights

**Netflix:** Executive Chairman (2023–present); Co-CEO (2020–2023); Co-Founder & CEO (1997–2020)
**Pure Software:** Founder & CEO (1991–1997)

### Other Roles and Boards

- California State Board of Education: President (2000–2004)
- Chairman of Powder Mountain ski resort
- On the boards of KIPP Foundation and Pahara Institute

### CEO Impact

- Turned the American DVD-by-mail service into a global 200-million-subscriber streaming-media business by seeing an opportunity where others saw a challenge. Instilled a corporate culture famous for radical transparency, feedback, and creativity.

### Fast Facts

- Ranked three times on *Fortune*'s Businessperson of the Year list
- Named twice in the *Time* 100 list of the most influential people in the world
- Appeared three times in *HBR*'s Top 100 CEOs
- Appeared nine times in *Barron's* World's Best CEOs
- Awarded the Henry Crown Leadership Award by the Aspen Institute, 2014
- Netflix ranked first in *HBR*'s Top 20 Business Transformations of the Last Decade, 2019

# SAM HAZEN
## HCA HEALTHCARE

**Revenue:** $65B
**Market cap:** $76B
**Employees:** 310k in 2 countries

### Career Highlights

**HCA Healthcare:** CEO (2019–present); President & Chief Operating Officer (2016–2019)

### Other Roles and Boards

- Held multiple executive roles at HCA Healthcare, including President of Operations and President of HCA Healthcare's Western Group
- On the boards of Nashville Health Care Council and the Federation of American Hospitals

### CEO Impact

- Led HCA Healthcare to become a leader in hospital operations and patient care, with 190 hospitals and approximately 2,400 ambulatory sites of care providing approximately 6% of all US inpatient hospital services. HCA Healthcare market cap has almost doubled, and revenue has increased by over 50% in his span as CEO so far over the past six years. Grew patient encounters in HCA Healthcare facilities from 35M in 2019 to approximately 44M in 2024. Increased market share from 25% in 2019 to 27% in 2022.

### Fast Facts

- Invested more than $300M in clinical education and training for nurses in 2023
- Expanded HCA Healthcare's scholarship programs to promote access to health care careers

## MARILLYN HEWSON
**LOCKHEED MARTIN**

Revenue: $68B
Market cap: $115B
Employees: 122k in 50+ countries

**Career Highlights**

Lockheed Martin: Chair (2014–2021); President & CEO (2013–2020)

**Other Roles and Boards**

- Lead Director of Johnson & Johnson
- On the board of Chevron
- Fellow of the American Institute of Aeronautics and Astronautics
- Member of the American Academy of Arts and Sciences, Trilateral Commission, Council on Foreign Relations, and Council of Chief Executives

**CEO Impact**

- Maintained a focus on the US defense contractor's mission to strengthen security and advance technology, while navigating tricky political waters and overcoming the challenge of being a woman in a male-dominated industry. Doubled EBITDA and more than tripled market cap.

**Fast Facts**

- Named to the *Time* 100 list of the World's Most Influential People, 2019
- Named in *Barron's* World's Best CEOs, 2019
- Named CEO of the Year by *Chief Executive Magazine*, 2018
- Appeared four times in *HBR*'s Top 100 CEOs
- Named in the top ten in *Fortune*'s Businessperson of the Year list, 2017
- *Fortune*'s Most Powerful Woman in Business, 2018 & 2019 (and ranked in the top four 2013–2019)
- Ranked twice in the top ten in *Forbes*' Most Powerful Women in the World

# KAZUO HIRAI
## SONY

Revenue: $87B
Market cap: $129B
Employees: 113k in 70+ countries

### Career Highlights

Sony: President & CEO (2012–2018); Chairman (2018–2019); Senior Advisor (2019–2024)

### CEO Impact

- Bucked Japanese corporate culture traditions with his style while turning around the media and consumer electronics giant by dramatically simplifying its portfolio. Increased operating margins by more than 900 basis points and restored the company to profitability after consecutive years of losses prior to his tenure.

### Fast Facts

- Named as one of the Top 500 Entertainment Business Leaders by *Variety*, 2017
- Received a Lifetime Achievement Award at the 66th Annual Technology & Engineering Emmy Awards in 2015

# HUBERT JOLY
## BEST BUY

Revenue: $43B
Market cap: $18B
Employees: 85k in 2 countries

**Career Highlights**

Best Buy: Chair (2015–2020); CEO (2012–2019)
Carlson Inc.: CEO (2008–2012)

**Other Roles and Boards**

- Senior Lecturer at Harvard Business School
- On the boards of Johnson & Johnson and Ralph Lauren
- Trustee of the Minneapolis Institute of Art and the New York Public Library

**CEO Impact**

- Moved the US consumer electronics and appliance retailer out of potential bankruptcy into a profitable company centered on customer experience and a strong employee culture. Achieved five consecutive years of same-store sales growth and a quadrupling of the stock price.

**Fast Facts**

- Included on the Thinkers50 list, a list of the world's most influential management thinkers, 2023
- Recipient of Stanley Hoffman Award from Sciences Po American Foundation, 2022
- Appeared in *HBR*'s Top 100 CEOs, 2018
- Named in *Barron's* World's Best CEOs, 2018
- Named four times in *Glassdoor*'s Top 100 CEOs in the US (once in the top ten)
- Made a Knight in the French Legion of Honor

# KV KAMATH
## ICICI BANK

Revenue: $19B
Market cap: $106B
Employees: 187k in 18 countries

### Career Highlights

ICICI Bank: Chair (2009–2015); CEO (1996–2009)
New Development Bank of BRICS countries: President (2015–2020)

### Other Roles and Boards

- Chair of the National Bank for Financing Infrastructure and Development and Jio Financial Services Limited
- On the board of Reliance Industries
- Senior Advisor at KKR India Financial Services

### CEO Impact

- Turned a small Indian wholesale lender into the largest private bank in the country through a combination of foresight, investment in technology, revolutionary talent management, and a desire to learn constantly. Delivered 33 percentage points of excess shareholder return relative to the sector while growing revenue more than twentyfold.

### Fast Facts

- Honored with the *Economic Times* Lifetime Achievement Award for Corporate Excellence, 2016
- Awarded the Padma Bhushan, 2008
- Named CEO of the Year by the *World HRD Congress*, 2007
- Named *Forbes Asia*'s Businessman of the Year, 2007

# GAIL KELLY
## WESTPAC

Revenue: $22B
Market cap: $70B
Employees: 35k in 8 countries

### Career Highlights

Westpac: CEO (2008–2015)
St. George Bank: CEO (2002–2007)

### Other Roles and Boards

- Author of *Live Lead Learn: My Stories of Life and Leadership* (2017)
- Adjunct Professor at the University of New South Wales
- Membership Committee Chair of the Bretton Woods Committee
- Ambassador for Women's Empowerment for CARE Australia
- On the boards of Singtel and UBS

### CEO Impact

- Made the Australian bank one of the world's most admired companies, while more than doubling market cap and skillfully steering it through the financial crisis through a relentless focus on customers. Championed diversity and inclusion, achieving goal of 40% women in the top 4,000 leadership roles.

### Fast Facts

- First female CEO of a major Australian bank
- Awarded an honorary Doctor of Business from the University of New South Wales, 2014
- Appeared in *Forbes'* Most Powerful Women in the World list for seven consecutive years, 2008–2014
- Ranked twice in the top twenty in the *Financial Times'* Top 50 Women in World Business, 2010–2011

# JØRGEN VIG KNUDSTORP
## LEGO

**Revenue:** $10B
**Market cap:** N/A
**Employees:** 28k in 40+ countries

### Career Highlights

**The LEGO Group:** President & CEO (2004–2016); Board Member (2017–present)
**LEGO Foundation:** Deputy Chair (2008–present)
**IMD School of Management:** Foundation Board Member (2006–present); Incoming Chair of the Supervisory and Foundation Boards (beginning 2026)

### Other Roles and Boards

- On the boards of Starbucks, Merlin Entertainments Limited, and Innovation Endeavors

### CEO Impact

- Turned the Danish family-owned firm into the world's most profitable toymaker, growing revenue fivefold and EBITDA sixteenfold. Centralized leadership, divested non-core assets, streamlined creativity, and embraced LEGO's adult consumers to reinvigorate the loss-making company.

### Fast Facts

- An AACSB Influential Leader Honoree, 2015
- Received the Committee for Economic Development's Global Leadership Award, 2015

## ARVIND KRISHNA
**IBM**

Revenue: $62B
Market cap: $203B
Employees: 282k in 175+ countries

### Career Highlights

IBM: Chair (2021–present); CEO (2020–present); Senior Vice President, Cloud and Cognitive Software (2019–2020); Senior Vice President, Hybrid Cloud & Director, IBM Research (2015–2019)

### Other Roles and Boards

- On the boards of Northrop Grumman, the Federal Reserve Bank of New York, and the US-India Strategic Partnership Forum

### CEO Impact

- Drove IBM's enterprise market leadership in hybrid cloud, AI, and quantum computing. Expanded and strengthened IBM's Partner Ecosystem. Created multiple billion-dollar books of business around strategic partnerships with companies like AWS, Microsoft, and others. Simplified IBM's go-to-market strategy and developed a unified client engagement model. Led 50+ acquisitions to strengthen IBM's portfolio and nearly doubled the company's market cap since 2020.

### Fast Facts

- Recipient of Hunt Scanlon's Excellence in Culture Award, 2024
- Recipient of the Yale Legend in Leadership Award, 2023
- Named by *Wired* magazine as "one of 25 geniuses who are creating the future of business," 2016

# RAMON LAGUARTA
**PEPSICO**

**Revenue:** $91B
**Market cap:** $211B
**Employees:** 318k with products sold in 200+ countries and territories

### Career Highlights

**PepsiCo:** CEO (2018–present); Chairman of the Board (2019–present); President (2017–2018); CEO of Europe & Sub-Saharan Africa (2015–2017)

### Other Roles and Boards

- Co-Chair of the World Economic Forum's Board of Stewards for the Food Systems Initiative
- On the board of Visa Inc.

### CEO Impact

- Pivoted the company toward accelerated growth, leading record productivity initiatives and a company-wide digital transformation, creating a high-performing employee culture, and launching PepsiCo Positive (pep+), the company's end-to-end strategic business transformation focused on creating sustainable growth and value, including efforts to reduce virgin plastic and expand the company's better-for-you product offering. Market cap has increased 41% over his tenure.

### Fast Facts

- Named one of *Barron's* Top CEOs, 2023
- Named one of *Fortune*'s World's 50 Greatest Leaders, 2018

# MAURICE LÉVY

## PUBLICIS

Revenue: $16B
Market cap: $27B
Employees: 103k in 50+ countries

### Career Highlights

Publicis: Emeritus Chairman (2024–present); Chair (1987–2024); CEO (1987–2017)

### Other Roles and Boards

- Cofounded the French Brain Institute (ICM)
- On the board of the Perse Center for Peace and Innovation
- Member of The Genesis Prize Advisory Board

### CEO Impact

- Turned a small French advertising company into an international marketing and communications giant by marrying a global outlook and a rich understanding of digitization with a local cultural nuance. Fueled by bold acquisitions, he grew revenue more than fortyfold and market cap one-hundredfold.

### Fast Facts

- Appointed a French Commander of the Legion of Honor and a Grand Officer of the National Order of Merit
- Inducted into the Advertising Hall of Fame by the American Advertising Federation (AAF), 2019
- Appeared twice in *HBR*'s Top 100 CEOs
- Received the International Leadership Award from the Anti-Defamation League, 2008

# BRIAN MOYNIHAN
## BANK OF AMERICA

Revenue: $99B
Market cap: $337B
Employees: 213k in 35 countries

### Career Highlights

Bank of America: Chair (2014–present); CEO (2010–present)

### Other Roles and Boards

- Chair of the World Economic Forum's International Business Council Stakeholder Capitalism Metrics Initiative, The Clearing House Association, and the Sustainable Markets Initiative, which was founded by His Majesty King Charles III
- Co-Chair of the American Heart Association CEO Roundtable
- Chancellor of the Corporation of Brown University
- Member of the advisory council for the Smithsonian National Museum of African American History and Culture
- On the boards of the Financial Services Forum, the Bank Policy Institute, the Business Roundtable, the Council on Competitiveness Board, and The Business Council

### CEO Impact

- Steered the bank through post-financial crisis recovery with a relentless focus on efficiency and organic growth, achieving consistent shareholder returns throughout. Positioned Bank of America as a technology powerhouse, increasing its patents to ~6,600, the most US patents of any financial services company in the country. More than doubled market cap since taking over as CEO in 2010.

### Fast Facts

- Named one of *Fortune*'s 100 Most Powerful People in Business, 2024
- Named one of *Barron's* Top CEOs, 2022
- Presented with the Business Committee Civic Leadership Award by The Metropolitan Museum of Art for commitment to and generous support of cultural institutions, 2022
- Bank of America named one of *Time*'s 100 Most Influential Companies, 2024
- Bank of America ranked four times on LinkedIn's Top 50 Companies in the US list

## SATYA NADELLA
### MICROSOFT

Revenue: $211B
Market cap: $3.1T
Employees: 221k in 30+ countries

**Career Highlights**

Microsoft: Chairman (2021–present); CEO (2014–present)

**Other Roles and Boards**

- Trustee of University of Chicago
- Member of The Business Council

**CEO Impact**

- Quickly steered Microsoft to areas of profitable growth when it was struggling to stay relevant, in part by fostering a corporate culture that called for a "learn-it-all" not "know-it-all" mindset. Has quadrupled EBITDA and grown market cap by nearly 10 times to make Microsoft the second most valuable public company in the world. This was the result of Nadella's focus on cloud and AI businesses.

**Fast Facts**

- Named as the "most admired" leader of the Fortune 500 CEOs, 2024
- Named *CNN*'s Business CEO of the Year, 2023
- Awarded the Padma Bhushan, the third highest civilian award in India, 2022
- Named *Financial Times*' Person of the Year, 2019
- Named *Fortune*'s Businessperson of the Year, 2019
- Appeared twice in the *Time* 100 list of the World's Most Influential People
- Appeared twice in *HBR*'s Top 100 CEOs (once in top 10)
- Appeared four times in *Barron's* World's Best CEOs

## SHANTANU NARAYEN
### ADOBE

Revenue: $19B
Market cap: $196B
Employees: 30k in 25+ countries

**Career Highlights**

**Adobe:** Chair (2017–present); CEO (2007–present)

**Other Roles and Boards**

- Vice-Chair of the US-India Strategic Partnership Forum
- On the board of Pfizer
- President Obama's Management Advisory Board member (2011–2017)

**CEO Impact**

- Pioneered cloud-based subscription services, transforming the company's business model from packaged products to software as a service, with revenues growing more than sixfold and market cap more than eightfold.

**Fast Facts**

- Awarded the Padma Shri by the President of India, 2019
- Recognized by *Fortune* as one of the 100 Most Powerful People in Business, 2024
- Named *Fortune*'s Businessperson of the Year, 2020
- Named *Economic Times*' Global Indian of the Year, 2018
- Has been recognized multiple times by *Barron's* as one of the World's Best CEOs

# FLEMMING ØRNSKOV, MD, MPH
## GALDERMA

Revenue: $4B
Market cap: $26B
Employees: 6k in 40 countries

### Career Highlights

Galderma: CEO (2019–present)
Shire: CEO (2013–2019)

### Other Roles and Boards

- Chair of Waters Corporation

### CEO Impact

- More than tripled revenue and market cap while expanding into 25 new countries—built on a vision to make Shire the world's leading rare-disease company. At Galderma, grew net sales 12% CAGR over 2019–2023 and led its CHF 2.3B IPO in 2024, IFR's 2024 EMEA IPO of the Year.

### Fast Facts

- Named in *Fierce Pharma*'s 25 Most Influential People in Biopharma, 2015
- Qualified as a medical doctor at the University of Copenhagen
- Earned a Master of Public Health from Harvard University School of Public Health and an MBA from INSEAD

## JIM OWENS
### CATERPILLAR

Revenue: $67B
Market cap: $175B
Employees: 113k in 25+ countries

### Career Highlights

**Caterpillar:** Chair & CEO (2004–2010)

### Other Roles and Boards

- On the board of the Peterson Institute for International Economics
- Member of the Council on Foreign Relations

### CEO Impact

- Dug the US industrial company out of stagnation with a clear strategic vision based on geographical and end market segments focus, performance objectives, product/service offerings, operational excellence, and rising employee involvement and satisfaction. Nearly doubled market cap and optimized the cost structure so the highly cyclical company could sustain profitability through the financial crisis.

### Fast Facts

- Member of the President's Economic Recovery Advisory Board, 2009
- Received the National Foreign Trade Council's World Trade Award, 2007

## DOUG PETERSON
**S&P GLOBAL**

Revenue: $12B
Market Cap: $154B
Employees: 40k in 35 countries

### Career Highlights
S&P Global: President & CEO (2013–2024)

### Other Roles and Boards
- On the boards of the National Bureau of Economic Research, UN Global Compact, Claremont McKenna College, Japan Society, and Paul Taylor Dance Company
- Member of the FDIC's Systemic Resolution Advisory Committee
- Co-leader of the World Bank Originate to Distribute Working Group

### CEO Impact
- Repositioned S&P Global from a media conglomerate to realize its vision of 'Powering Global Markets' with data, analytics, and benchmarks, and a strong emphasis on purpose, values, and people. Led S&P through the $44B acquisition and integration of HIS Markit. Elevated sustainability to become a cornerstone of the company's strategy. Acquired Kensho, an AI company, in 2018, positioning S&P to be a leader in data and GenAI. Revenue more than doubled and market cap increased more than nine times during his tenure.

### Fast Facts
- Received the Carnegie Hall Medal of Excellence in recognition of his remarkable commitment to philanthropy and his dedication and partnership with the arts, 2023
- Led a workstream of the G7's Impact Taskforce to mobilize private capital through consistent global standards to measure, value, and account for sustainability, 2021
- Recognized as one of *HBR*'s Top CEOs, 2019

# KEN POWELL
## GENERAL MILLS

**Revenue:** $20B
**Market cap:** $35B
**Employees:** 35k in 25+ countries

### Career Highlights

**General Mills:** Chairman & CEO (2007–2017)
**Cereal Partners Worldwide:** CEO (1999–2004)

### Other Roles and Boards

- Chair of Partners in Food Solutions, a nonprofit dedicated to strengthening food security and increasing economic development across Africa
- On the boards of Medtronic and Carlson

### CEO Impact

- Responded to changing customer preferences to move the US consumer foods giant toward healthier products, while also embedding a deep understanding of local cultural context. Almost doubled market cap and delivered more than 5 percentage points of excess shareholder return relative to the sector.

### Fast Facts

- Received the Keystone Policy Center's Founders Award, 2016
- Received the Committee for Economic Development's Corporate Citizenship Award, 2013
- Topped *Glassdoor*'s America's Most Beloved CEOs list, 2010

## STEPHEN SCHWARZMAN
### BLACKSTONE

Revenue: $8B
Market cap: $211B
Employees: 5k in 15+ countries

**Career Highlights**

Blackstone: Chairman, CEO, & Co-Founder (1985–present)

**Other Roles and Boards**

- Founding Trustee and Co-Chairman of the Board of Trustees of Schwarzman Scholars
- Chairman Emeritus of the John F. Kennedy Center for the Performing Arts
- On the board of the Asia Society, New York-Presbyterian Hospital, and New York Public Library
- On the advisory board of the School of Economics and Management at Tsinghua University, Beijing
- Trustee of The Frick Collection

**CEO Impact**

- Played a transformative role in building Blackstone's reputation as a global leader in private equity, real estate, credit, and alternative investments. Under his leadership, Blackstone's Assets Under Management had grown to over $1.1T by 2024, establishing dominance across asset classes.

**Fast Facts**

- Appointed Honorary Knight of the British Empire (KBE), 2024
- Author of *What It Takes: Lessons in the Pursuit of Excellence*, a *New York Times* bestseller, 2019
- Named one of *Barron's* World's Best CEOs, 2019
- On *Forbes'* Top 50 Most Powerful People, 2018
- Donated over $1B in charitable giving, including to educational institutions such as Yale, MIT, and Oxford

# ROBERTO SETÚBAL
## ITAÚ UNIBANCO

**Revenue:** $32B
**Market cap:** $49B
**Employees:** 93k in 18 countries

### Career Highlights

Itaú Unibanco: Co-Chair (2017–present); CEO (1994–2016)

### Other Roles and Boards

- Member of the Federal Reserve Bank of New York, International Advisory Committee

### CEO Impact

- Transformed the Brazilian bank into a top-ten global financial institution, masterminding a series of acquisitions to expand both geographically and into investment banking. Grew revenue twenty-fivefold and market cap more than thirtyfold.

### Fast Facts

- Appeared twice in *HBR*'s Top 100 CEOs (twice in top 5)
- Named *Euromoney*'s Banker of the Year, 2011

# JOSHUA SILVERMAN
## ETSY, INC.

Revenue: $3B
Market cap: $6B
Employees: 2k in 6 countries

### Career Highlights

**Etsy:** CEO (2017–present); Board Member (2016–present)
**American Express:** President of Consumer Products and Services (2011–2015)
**Skype:** CEO (2008–2010)

### Other Roles and Boards

- On the board of Shake Shack

### CEO Impact

- Under Josh's leadership, Etsy has fortified its reputation as the home for creativity and self-expression and more than doubled its community to 8M sellers and 95M buyers. With a focus on financial discipline, Josh has ushered the company through a period of significant revenue and profit growth and heavily invested in AI and machine learning technology to enhance the shopping experience. These improvements, coupled with Josh's vision for keeping commerce human, have created more joyful shopping experiences, made it easier for shoppers to find items that are special to them, and created economic opportunities for millions of creative entrepreneurs around the world.

### Fast Facts

- Selected as a Henry Crown Fellow by The Aspen Institute

# BRAD SMITH
## INTUIT

**Revenue:** $16B
**Market cap:** $176B
**Employees:** 18k in 7 countries

### Career Highlights

**Intuit:** Chair (2016–2022); CEO (2008–2018)
**Marshall University:** President (2022–present)

### Other Roles and Boards

- On the boards of JPMorgan Chase, Amazon, and Humana
- Founded the Wing 2 Wing Foundation to advance education and entrepreneurship in overlooked areas of the country

### CEO Impact

- Changed the American software giant's model from desktop to cloud and focused on delighting customers through his mission to "power prosperity around the world." Doubled revenue and grew market cap fivefold.

### Fast Facts

- Appeared twice in *HBR*'s Top 100 CEOs
- Ranked twice in *Fortune*'s Businessperson of the Year list (once in top 10)
- Served on the President's Advisory Council on Financial Capability for Young Americans, 2014–2015

## ROBERT F. SMITH
**VISTA EQUITY PARTNERS**

AUM: $100B+
Revenue: N/A
Market cap: N/A
Employees: 700+ globally

**Career Highlights**

Vista Equity Partners: Founder, Chairman, & CEO (2000–present)

**Other Roles and Boards**

- Founder of the Student Freedom Initiative
- Founding Director and President of internXL
- Founding Partner of the REFORM Alliance, World Economic Forum EDISON Alliance, and Fund II Foundation
- Chair of Carnegie Hall
- On the boards of the Southern Communities Initiative, Robert F. Kennedy Human Rights, NAF, Columbia Business School, and Grand Slam Track

**CEO Impact**

- As founder-CEO, built Vista into a global technology investor that specializes in enterprise software. Today, Vista has more than $100B in AUM and manages a portfolio of 85+ software companies that provide mission-critical solutions to millions of customers around the world.

**Fast Facts**

- Recipient of Realizing the Dream's The Dreamer Award, 2024
- Awarded the George H. W. Bush Points of Light Award, 2023
- Recognized by *Time* as one of the 100 Most Influential People, 2020
- Recipient of the Carnegie Medal for Philanthropy, 2019
- Named one of *Bloomberg*'s 50 People Who Defined the Year, 2019
- Named one of *Forbes*' 100 Greatest Living Business Minds, 2017

# LIP-BU TAN
## CADENCE DESIGN SYSTEMS

Revenue: $4B
Market cap: $82B
Employees: 11k in 30+ countries

**Career Highlights**

**Cadence Design Systems:** CEO (2009–2021); Chair (2021–2023)
**Walden International:** Chair (1984–present)
**Walden Catalyst Ventures:** Founding Managing Partner (2020–present)

**Other Roles and Boards**

- Chair of SambaNova Systems, Credo, Artera.ai, Greenstone Biosciences, and Rivos Inc.
- On the boards of Schneider Electric, Green Hills Software, Carnegie Mellon University, and Fuller Theological Seminary
- Member of MIT School of Engineering Dean's Advisory Council

**CEO Impact**

- Turned around this troubled US electronic design company by adopting a singular focus on the customer (mostly semiconductor and chip manufacturers) and expanding into new markets. Improved operating margins by over 30% and grew market cap twentyfold.

**Fast Facts**

- Awarded Robert N. Noyce Award, Semiconductor Industry Association's highest honor, 2022
- Received the Global Semiconductor Association's Dr. Morris Chang Exemplary Leadership Award, 2016
- Cadence named six times in *Fortune*'s 100 Best Companies to Work For, 2015–2020

# PETER WENNINK
## ASML

Revenue: $30B
Market cap: $276B
Employees: 42k+ in 15 countries

**Career Highlights**

ASML: CEO (2013–2024)

**Other Roles and Boards**

- Chair of the Eindhoven University of Technology Supervisory Board
- Chair of the Heineken Board
- Co-Chair of the Advisory Committee of the Dutch National Growth Fund
- On the supervisory board of VDL Groep

**CEO Impact**

- Spearheaded ASML's prominence in the global semiconductor equipment market, particularly in EUV lithography technology, making ASML a cornerstone of the chip making supply chain. Under his tenure, ASML's revenue grew more than fourfold, and its market cap more than sevenfold.

**Fast Facts**

- Appointed a Grand Officer of the Order of Orange-Nassau
- Named one of *Fortune*'s Businesspersons of the Year, 2020

# MICHAEL WIRTH
## CHEVRON CORPORATION

Revenue: $197B
Market cap: $260B
Employees: 46k in 25+ countries

### Career Highlights

Chevron: Chairman & CEO (2018–present)

### Other Roles and Boards

- On the boards of the American Petroleum Institute and the National Football Foundation
- Member of the World Economic Forum International Business Council, American Heart Association CEO Roundtable, Business Council, and the American Society of Corporate Executives

### CEO Impact

- Balanced the difficult equation of growing Chevron's traditional energy business while investing in technologies to meet the demand for new lower carbon energies. Under Wirth, Chevron committed ~$1B and invested in more than 30 companies that support low-carbon innovations, and reduced the methane intensity of its oil and gas operations by more than 50% since 2016.

### Fast Facts

- Awarded the Distinguished Engineering Alumni Award, 2010, and the University Medal, 2014, by Colorado University

## ACKNOWLEDGMENTS

Beyond the CEOs we interviewed, we also thank our many partner colleagues at McKinsey, who are too numerous to mention by name, for introducing us to the CEOs we interviewed and sharing their own learnings. Without these trusted counselors, we wouldn't have had the same level of access to these incredible leaders.

There were countless colleagues working behind the scenes without whom the book you hold in your hands wouldn't be possible. Special callouts for their contributions to the book's content go to: Eman Ahmed, Shahnaz Ajani, Kemi Amurawaiye, Ivo Bozon, Luis Cerro, Riyana Chakraborty, Jalen Daniels, Farah Dilber, Jodi Elkins, Blair Epstein, John Kelleher, Maliha Khan, Sara Messina, Alice Ding Nelson, Selin Neseliler, John Nixon, Rutendo Njawaya, Amuche Okeke-Agba, James Oliver, Michelle Rose, Youssef Sabek, Awadhi Saxena, Amy Slaughter, Sander Smits, Jaya Todi, Jen Whitaker, Lindsey Wilcox, Kerone Wint, Isabelle Wisco, Laeticia Yang, Lorelei Yang, and Jessica Zehren.

For their editorial support we'd like express our gratitude to Brian Dumaine, Claire Holland, Rick Tetzeli, and especially Scribner's Rick Horgan, who expertly guided us and made us better through the writing process. We further extend our appreciation to Uli Knorzer for his illustrations that accompany the CEO biographies in Appendix B. Also, a special thank you to Raju Narisetti, the leader of McKinsey's

Global Publishing group, for encouraging and enabling us as we've aspired to make the role of the CEO—and how to excel in it—a unique and distinctive knowledge domain.

Most important, we are grateful to our families for putting up with the years of "nights and weekends" work that went into writing this book. We all have full-time jobs serving clients at McKinsey that didn't let up during the writing process, and without our families' support and forgiveness for the seemingly unending time away from the home front, this project wouldn't have been possible.

Lastly, we thank you, our readers, for coming on this journey with us. We welcome any feedback you're willing to share. You can reach us at CEO_Excellence@McKinsey.com.

# NOTES

### CHAPTER ONE
### Stepping Up: Becoming a High-Potential CEO Candidate

1. Unless otherwise noted, all quotations from leaders in this book come from unpublished interviews conducted as part of McKinsey research or from Carolyn Dewar et al., *CEO Excellence: The Six Mindsets That Distinguish the Best Leaders from the Rest*, Scribner, 2022.

2. "End of the journey / new beginnings," "Everest Climbing Routes, Camps, Obstacles, Landmarks, the Death Zone and Summiting," Facts and Details, updated February 2022, https://factsanddetails.com/south-asia/Nepal/Himalayas/entry-7877.html, February 9, 2023.

3. Samantha Saperstein, host, *Women on the Move*, "General Motors Head Mary Barra Talks Leadership and Tips for Women," JPMorgan Chase, October 7, 2021, https://womenonthemove.podbean.com/e/general-motors-head-mary-barra-talks-leadership-and-tips-for-women/.

4. Saperstein, "General Motors Head Mary Barra Talks Leadership and Tips for Women."

5. Ola Svenson, "Are We All Less Risky and More Skillful Than Our Fellow Drivers?," *Acta Psychologica* 47, no. 2 (1981), https://doi.org/10.1016/0001-6918(81)90005-6.

6. Mark D. Alicke and Olesya Govorun, "The Better-Than-Average Effect," in Mark D. Alicke et al., eds., *The Self in Social Judgment* (New York: Psychology Press, 2005).

7. Michael Ross and Fiore Sicoly, "Egocentric Biases in Availability and Attribution," *Journal of Personality and Social Psychology* 37, no. 3 (1979), https://doi.org/10.1037/0022-3514.37.3.322.

8. "The route," "Everest Climbing Routes, Camps, Obstacles, Landmarks, the Death Zone and Summiting."

9. "End of the journey / new beginnings," "Everest Climbing Routes, Camps, Obstacles, Landmarks, the Death Zone and Summiting."

## CHAPTER TWO
### Starting Strong: Making Your CEO Transition a Catalyst for Renewal

1. Joubin Mirzadegan, host, *Grit*, "#218 CEO Etsy, Josh Silverman: Second Acts," Kleiner Perkins, November 25, 2024, https://open.spotify.com/episode/6s8fbbSM7DX60t4Wf8zqoi.

2. Ibid.

3. Chris Bradley et al., "Strategy to Beat the Odds," *McKinsey Quarterly*, February 13, 2018.

4. Mirzadegan, "#218 CEO Etsy, Josh Silverman: Second Acts."

## CHAPTER THREE
### Staying Ahead: How the Best CEOs Continually Improve Performance

1. R. Ray Wang, "Research Summary: Sneak Peeks from Constellation's Futurist Framework and 2014 Outlook on Digital Disruption," Constellation Research, February 18, 2014, https://www.constellationr.com/blog-news/research-summary-sneak-peeks-constellations-futurist-framework-and-2014-outlook-digital.

2. Alexandra Zendrian, "In Pictures: The Top Gun CEOs," *Forbes*, June 23, 2009.

3. Monica Langley, "Inside J.P. Morgan's Blunder," *Wall Street Journal*, May 18, 2012.

4. Vik Malhotra and Asheet Mehta, hosts, *Inside the Strategy Room*, "Voices of CEO Excellence: Morgan Stanley's James Gorman," McKinsey, July 22, 2022, https://www.mckinsey.com/capabilities/strategy-and-corporate-finance/our-insights/voices-of-ceo-excellence-morgan-stanleys-james-gorman.

5. Diane Brady, "Salesforce's Marc Benioff Bashes Microsoft—Again," *Fortune*, December 19, 2024.

6. Daniel Kahneman, *Thinking, Fast and Slow* (New York: Farrar, Straus and Giroux, 2011).

7. Andrew S. Grove, *Only the Paranoid Survive: How to Exploit the Crisis Points That Challenge Every Company* (New York: Currency, 1996).

8. Daniel Kahneman et al., eds., *Judgment Under Uncertainty: Heuristics and Biases* (Cambridge, UK: Cambridge University Press, 1982).

9. Sanjay Kalavar and Mihir Mysore, "Are You Prepared for a Corporate Crisis?," *McKinsey Quarterly*, April 17, 2017.

CHAPTER FOUR
## Sending It Forward: Successfully Transitioning Out of the CEO Role

1. David Gendelman, "Why Can't the U.S. Relay Team Figure Out How to Pass a Baton?," Intelligencer, *New York*, August 5, 2021.

2. Claudio Fernández-Aráoz et al., "The High Cost of Poor Succession Planning," *Harvard Business Review*, May-June 2021.

3. Ben Cohen, "Bob Iger Is Back at Disney to Fix His One Big Failure: Succession," *Wall Street Journal*, December 1, 2022.

CONCLUSION
## The Future of the CEO Role

1. Natalie Walters, "The Social Media Platforms That Hit 100 Million Users Fastest," The Motley Fool, April 21, 2019, https://www.fool.com/investing/2019/01/20/the-social-media-platforms-that-hit-100-million-us.aspx.

2. Krystal Hu, "ChatGPT Sets Record for Fastest-Growing User Base - Analyst Note," Reuters, February 2, 2023, https://www.reuters.com/technology/chatgpt-sets-record-fastest-growing-user-base-analyst-note-2023-02-01/.

3. "Navigating the Currents of Disruption I Fortune," posted September 24, 2018, by *Fortune* magazine, YouTube, https://www.youtube.com/watch?v=ZDH6bW1j1N4.

4. Aneel Chima and Ron Gutman, "What It Takes to Lead Through an Era of Exponential Change," *Harvard Business Review*, October 29, 2020; Lee Shapiro, "The Unprecedented Pace of Change," *Forbes*, February 25, 2021; PJ Bain, "How to Thrive in the Era of Uncertainty," *Forbes*, October 26, 2023.

5. "Businesses Anticipate Unprecedented Rate of Change in 2024, New Accenture 'Pulse of Change Index' Shows," Accenture, January 12, 2024, https://newsroom.accenture.com/news/2024/businesses-anticipate-unprecedented-rate-of-change-in-2024-new-accenture-pulse-of-change-index-shows.

6. Ani Petrosyan, "Internet Usage Worldwide - Statistics & Facts," Statista, April 11, 2025, https://www.statista.com/topics/1145/internet-usage-worldwide/#topicOverview.

7. Barry Libert, "Leaders Need AI to Keep Pace with the Data Explosion," *Forbes*, March 26, 2019.

8. *The Further Enlargement of the EU: Threat or Opportunity?*, Authority of the House of Lords, November 23, 2006, https://publications.parliament.uk/pa/ld200506/ldselect/ldeucom/273/273.pdf.

# INDEX

Note: Italicized page numbers indicate names or concepts that appear in charts and graphs.

## A

accountability, of new CEOs, 39–40
acting, listening before, 44–47
Adidas, 72, 159
Adobe, 11, 29, 39, 46, 53–54, 73, 77, 88, 173. *see also* Narayen, Shantanu
Aesop's fable, 57–58
Allianz SE, 39, 42, 48, 141
American Express, 94, 145
America's 100 Most Innovative Leaders *(Forbes)*, 9
anchoring heuristic, 65–66
Anthem. *see* Elevance Health
Aon, 50, 61, 144
Apple, 109
Archimedes, 107
Are You Asking the Right Questions?, *43*
Asch, Solomon, 47
Asher-Topilsky, Lilach, 49, 78, 140
ASML, 11–12, 25, 26, 48, 64, 95, 184
authenticity
  gut checking motivation and, 32
  meaning-making and, 110
  selection process and, 34, 36

## B

balance
  dichotomies considered for, *111–12*
  of work and personal life, 26
Banco Itaú, 71
Bank of America, 70–71, 75, 171
Barra, Mary, 21–22, 27, 29, 76
*Barron's*, Top 30 CEOs, 9
Barton, Dominic, 70
Bäte, Oliver, 39, 42, 48, 141
Beatles, 97–98
Benioff, Marc, 64
Best Buy, 55, 73–74, 164
"best CEO" lists, 9
"big ball," 51–55
BlackRock, Inc., 69, 73, 151
Blackstone, 27, 178
Blanchard, Kenneth, 134
Blankfein, Lloyd, 84
blind spots of CEOs, assessing, 12–18, *13–15*
Bloch, Ray, 97
Board Effectiveness (reflection exercise #4), 126–27, *128–29*
Boeing, 74
Bohr, Niels, 97
Boudreaux, Gail, 11, 27, 40, 45, 49, 62, 89, 142

193

BP, 74
Brabeck-Letmathe, Peter, 63, 143
Bridges, William, 39
Buckley, William F., Jr., 97

C
Cadence Design Systems, 89, 183
Campbell, Bill, 86
Campbell Soup supermarket experiment, 65–66
candor, 49
Case, Greg, 50, 61, 144
Caterpillar, 82, 87, 92, 175
CEO biographies, 139–85. *see also individual names of CEOs*
   about, 139
   Asher-Topilsky, 140
   Bäte, 141
   Boudreaux, 142
   Brabeck-Letmathe, 143
   Case, 144
   Chenault, 145
   Culp, 146
   Cutler, 147
   Davis, 148
   Dell, 149
   Dimon, 150
   Fink, 151
   Fisher, 152
   Frazier, 153
   Friedman, 154
   George, 155
   Gorman, 156
   Grossman, 157
   Gupta, 158
   Hainer, 159
   Hastings, 160
   Hazen, 161
   Hewson, 162
   Hirai, 163
   Joly, 164
   Kamath, 165
   Kelly, 166
   Knudstorp, 167
   Krishna, 168
   Laguarta, 169
   Lévy, 170
   Moynihan, 171
   Nadella, 172
   Narayen, 173
   Ørnskov, 174
   Owens, 175
   Peterson, 176
   Powell, 177
   Schwarzman, 178
   Setúbal, 179
   Silverman, 180
   Smith (Brad), 181
   Smith (Robert F.), 182
   Tan, 183
   Wennink, 184
   Wirth, 185
CEO councils, 62
*CEO Excellence* (Dewar, Keller, and Malhotra)
   audience of, 8
   *CEO for All Seasons* as follow-up to, 6, 10, 11
   on differentiated perspective, 97–98
   on influencing behavior change, 16
   on six demands of CEO role, 13, 25, 105
*CEO for All Seasons* (Dewar, Keller, Malhotra, and Strovink)
   approach to, 8–12, *11*
   goals of book, 6–8
CEO leadership cycle, 3–19
   blind spots of CEOs, assessing, 12–18, *13–15*
   book's goals for, 6–8
   former CEOs in executive chairman role, 91–92

as four-season journey, 3–5, 105
identifying best CEOs, 8–12, *11*
impact of CEOs and, 18–19
leading through leaders, 107
six demands of CEOs, 13, 25, 105
tenure, average length, 83
CEO leadership cycle, becoming high-potential CEO, 21–37
  aspiring to CEO role, 21–22, 37
  elevating your perspective for role, 26–29
  gut checking motivation and expectations for role, 23–26, *24*, 32
  humility and importance to, 30–33
  new roles before CEO promotion, 88
  selection process and, 33–37
  as "spring" cycle of CEOs, 4, 5
CEO leadership cycle, early years, 39–56
  blind spots during, 16, *17*
  expectations for, 39–40, 55–56
  first impression importance to, 47–51
  impact of, 56
  listening before taking action, 44–47
  perspective and thinking beyond oneself for, 41–44, *43*
  playing "big ball" for effectiveness, 51–55
  as renewal opportunity for organization, 40–41
  "sophomore slump" during, 7, 10
  as "summer" cycle of CEOs, 4
CEO leadership cycle, mid-tenure years, 57–79
  avoiding complacency in, 57–60, 78–79
  blind spots during, 16–17, *17*
  complacency in, 7, 10
  as "fall" cycle of CEOs, 4
  future-proofing for crises during, 74–78
  learning enhancement for, 60–65
  outsider's perspective for, 65–70
  S-curve strategy for, 70–74
  "The Tortoise and the Hare" (Aesop's fable) as analogy to, 57–58
CEO leadership cycle, late-tenure years, 81–96
  blind spots during, 17, *17*
  handoff as graceful, 89–92
  relay race analogy, 81–82, 96
  shaping post-CEO portfolio, 93–96
  succession planning, 86–89
  timing of departure, 83–85
  transition importance, 81–83
  transition stages, after new CEO is announced, 90–91
  as "winter" cycle of CEOs, 4, 5
CEO role, future of, 97–112
  anticipating future possibilities for next practices, 106–12
  change in business world and, 98–106
  dichotomies balanced by leaders, *111–12*
  perspective needed for, 97–98, 112
"CEO's Journey Is a 3-Act Play, The" (Nohria), 7
*CEOWORLD*, Most Influential CEOs, 9
change
  future of CEO role and change in business world, 98–106
  influencing behavior change, 16
  S-curve strategy for, 70–74
  transition vs., 41

ChatGPT, 98
Chenault, Ken, 94, 145
Chevron Corporation, 28, 62, 69, 75, 104, 185
Cincinnati Children's Hospital Medical Center (CCHMC), 23, 25, 32, 35, 83, 90, 91, 95, 152. *see also* Fisher, Michael
climate change and sustainability, 100, 101, 102–3
coaches, perspective of, 31
complacency, avoiding, 57–60, 78–79. *see also* CEO leadership cycle, mid-tenure years
confirmation bias, 65–66
consumer behavior, change in, 100, 103
COO, selection process and, 36
councils of CEOs, 62
COVID-19 pandemic, 11, 77, 99, 100
crises, future-proofing for, 74–78
critics, perspective of, 63
Culp, Larry, 53, 54, 56, 146
Culture Change (reflection exercise #2), 118–19, *120–21*
culture of organization. *see* politics and organizational culture
curiosity, 108–9
Cutler, Sandy, 51, 147

**D**

Davis, Richard, 49, 78, 148
DBS Bank (DBS Group), 47, 86–87, 158
Decca Records, 97–98
decisiveness, 109
Deepwater Horizon oil spill, 74
Dell, Michael, 31, 66, 108, 149
Dell Technologies, 31, 66, 149

demographic shift, 101, 103–4
Dewar, Carolyn
  *CEO Excellence*, 6, 8, 10, 11, 13, 16, 25, 97, 105 (*see also CEO Excellence* (Dewar, Keller, and Malhotra))
  *CEO for All Seasons*, 6–8
Dimon, Jamie, 11, 45, 54, 59, 64, 70, 150
Direction Setting (reflection exercise #1), 114–15, *116–17*
Disney, 63
diversity, equity, and inclusion (DEI), 101, 103
divisional CEOs, selection process and, 36
Do You Really Want to Be a CEO? (sustainable mindset), 23–25, *24*. *see also* CEO leadership cycle, becoming high-potential CEO

**E**

early years in CEO role. *see* CEO leadership cycle, early years
Eaton Corporation, 51, 147
economic value
  CEOs and creation of, 7
  excess TRS (total financial return to shareholders), 9–10, *11*
  global economics and geopolitics, change in, 99, 102
  questions to ask for outsider's perspective, 66–68
*Ed Sullivan Show, The* (television show), 97
effectiveness, playing "big ball" for, 51–55. *see also* reflection exercises; self-assessment by CEOs
Einstein, Albert, 44, 108, 118

Elevance Health, 11, 27, 40, 45, 49, 62, 89, 142
employees. *see* talent management
Enron, 102
environmental, social, and governance (ESG) investments, 100, 103
Equifax, 75
Etsy, Inc., 22, 42, 43–44, 51–52, 61, 180
Evite, 42
excess TRS (total financial return to shareholders), 9–10, *11*
exercises. *see* reflection exercises
experience, self-assessment of, 30–31

**F**

Facebook, 98
"fall" cycle of CEOs, 4. *see also* CEO leadership cycle, mid-tenure years
"finish the job" notion, 88–89
Fink, Larry, 69, 151
first impression, importance of, 47–51
Fisher, Michael
 biography of, 152
 on early career of CEOs, 35
 on expectations of aspiring CEOs, 23, 25
 on humility of aspiring CEOs, 32
 on late career of CEOs, 83, 90, 91, 95
"flag planters," 29
*Forbes* magazine
 America's 100 Most Innovative Leaders, 9
 on Beatles, 97
 Forbes Global 2000, 74
 World's Most Powerful Women of 2024, 11

*Fortune* magazine
 Fortune 500 (2000), 58
 Most Powerful Women in Business, 9
four-season journey of CEOs, 3–5, 105, 113. *see also* CEO leadership cycle
Frazier, Ken, 42–43, 54, 75–76, 78, 153
Friedman, Adena
 on aspiring CEOs, 31
 biography of, 154
 on early career CEOs, 16, 42, 45, 46, 50
 on middle career CEOs, 75
future possibilities, anticipating, 106–12
future-proofing for crises, 74–78

**G**

Galderma, 53, 60–61, 174
General Electric (GE), 53, 54, 56, 146
General Mills, 26, 29, 62, 177
General Motors (GM), 21–22, 27, 29, 76
George, Bill, 23, 64–65, 72, 84–85, 96, 155
George, Penny, 96
"getting off the dance floor and going to the balcony" (elevating perspective), 26–29
"Goldilocks" format, 7–8
Goldman Sachs, 84
Gorman, James, 46–47, 59, 156
Grossman, Robert, 42, 50–51, 74, 88, 157
Grove, Andy, 66
Gupta, Piyush, 47, 86–87, 158

## H

Hainer, Herbert, 72, 159
handoff. *see* CEO leadership cycle, late-tenure years
*Harvard Business Review*, 7
  "The CEO's Journey Is a 3-Act Play" (Nohria), 7
  Top 100 CEOs, 9
Hastings, Reed, 48, 76, 160
Hayward, Tony, 74
Hazen, Sam, 10, 27, 40, 63, 82, 161
HCA Healthcare, 10, 27, 40, 63, 82, 161
headhunters, 33–35
heart paddles analogy, 70
Heifetz, Ronald, 26
Hersey, Paul, 134
heuristic, 65–66
Hewson, Marillyn, 45, 48, 162
Hildebrand, Claudius, 7
Hillary, Edmund, 21
Hirai, Kazuo, 84, 163
hiring of CEOs, internal vs. external, 36–37
Holmes, Oliver Wendell, Jr., 107
horse-racing analogy, 30
human resources (HR)
  Barra in role of, 22, 27, 29
  succession planning with, 86–87
humility, 30–33, 43, 78

## I

IBM, 12, 17, 25, 49–50, 63, 76–77, 87, 168. *see also* Krishna, Arvind
ICICI Bank, 93–94, 165
IDB, 78
immigration, 101, 104
industry perspective
  inter-industry councils of CEOs, 62
  inter-industry perspective, 63
  stepping up to CEO role and, 27–28
Instagram, 98
Intel, 65
intensity of effort, 70
internet, change due to, 99, 102, 103
interviews, selection process for CEOs, 33–37
Intuit, 30, 32, 61–64, 69, 77, 85, 86, 91, 92, 94–95, 181. *see also* Smith, Brad
investors, perspective of, 62
Israel Discount Bank, 49, 140
Itaú Unibanco, 69, 71, 179

## J

Jobs, Steve, 109
Joly, Hubert, 55, 73–74, 164
*Journey of Leadership, The* (Strovink et al.), 6
JPMorgan Chase's (JPMC), 11, 45, 54, 59, 64, 70, 150

## K

Kahneman, Daniel, 65, 71–72
Kamath, KV, 93–94, 165
Keillor, Garrison, 15
Keller, Scott
  *CEO Excellence*, 6, 8, 10, 11, 13, 16, 25, 97, 105 (*see also CEO Excellence* (Dewar, Keller, and Malhotra))
  *CEO for All Seasons*, 6–8
Kelly, Gail
  on aspiring CEOs, 28, 31
  authors' interview of, 11
  biography of, 166
  on early career CEOs, 51, 54
  on middle career CEOs, 84, 87, 93
King, Martin Luther, Jr., 110–11

knowledge, self-assessment of, 31
Knudstorp, Jørgen Vig, 51, 52, 61, 167
Krishna, Arvind
    authors' interview of, 12
    biography, 168
    on early career of CEOs, 49–50
    on learning from criticism, 63
    on middle career of CEOs, 17, 25, 76–77
    on succession planning, 87

**L**
Lafley, A. G., 49
Laguarta, Ramon, 26, 41, 59, 73, 94, 169
Lake Wobegon Effect, 15
leadership cycle. *see* CEO leadership cycle
leadership skill, self-assessment of, 31
learning
    enhancement of, for mid-tenure years, 60–65
    institutionalizing, 108–9
LEGO, 51, 52, 61, 167
Lévy, Maurice, 72–73, 170
Lewin, Kurt, 40–41
*Life Cycle of a CEO, The* (Hildebrand and Stark), 7
Linsky, Marty, 26
listening, before taking action, 44–47
Lockheed Martin, 45, 48, 162
Lombardi, Vince, 35
lottery ticket effect, 71–72

**M**
Malhotra, Vikram
    *CEO Excellence*, 6, 8, 10, 11, 13, 16, 25, 97, 105 (*see also CEO Excellence* (Dewar, Keller, and Malhotra))
    *CEO for All Seasons*, 6–8

McKinsey & Company
    about, 195–97
    Barton on intensity of effort, 70
    on CEO performance, 46
    focus of, 3
    Global Institute (research arm), 99
meaning, making, 110
Medtronic, 23, 64–65, 72, 84–85, 96, 155
Merck, 42–43, 54, 75–76, 78, 153
Microsoft, 82, 172
mid-tenure years as CEO. *see* CEO leadership cycle, mid-tenure years
Moore, Gordon, 66
moral reasoning, 110–11
Morgan Stanley, 46–47, 59, 156
Most Influential CEOs *(CEOWORLD)*, 9
Most Powerful Women in Business *(Fortune)*, 9
motivation
    first impressions and understanding "why," 48
    gut checking motivation and expectations for role, 23–26, *24*
    Stakeholder Engagement (reflection exercise #5) and understanding "why," 130–31, *132–33*
Mount Everest analogy, 21–22, 23, 33, 37
Moynihan, Brian, 70–71, 75, 171
Muilenburg, Dennis, 74
Mulcahy, Anne, 93
Munoz, Oscar, 75

**N**
Nadella, Satya, 82, 172
Narayen, Shantanu
    authors' interview of, 11
    biography of, 173

Narayen, Shantanu (*cont.*)
  on early career of CEOs, 39, 46, 53–54
  on "flag planters," 29
  on late career of CEOs, 88
  on mid career of CEOs, 73, 77
Nasdaq, 16, 31, 42, 45, 46, 50, 75, 154. *see also* Friedman, Adena
Nestlé, 63, 143
Netflix, 48, 76, 160
*New York* magazine, 81
next practices, anticipating future possibilities for, 106–12. *see also* CEO role, future of
Noah, Ray, 81
Nohria, Nitin, 7
Norgay, Tenzing, 21
"no," saying, 53, 109
NYU Langone Health, 42, 50–51, 74, 88, 157

O

*One Minute Manager, The* (Blanchard), 134
operating rhythm, 52, 54
organizational culture. *see* politics and organizational culture
organizational perspective
  questions for outsider's perspective, 68
  self-assessment by CEOs vs., 16
  stepping up to CEO role and, 27, 28
Ørnskov, Flemming, 53, 60–61, 174
outsider's perspective, 65–70
Owens, Jim, 82, 87, 92, 175

P

paradox, embracing, 111
PepsiCo, 26, 41, 59, 73, 94, 169
Personal Leadership Effectiveness (reflection exercise #6), 134–35, *136–37*
perspective
  CEO role future and, 97–98, 112
  councils of CEOs from multiple industries, 62
  of critics, 63
  Direction Setting (reflection exercise #1), 114–15, *116–17*
  elevating, 26–29
  industry perspective, 27–28
  inter-industry perspective, 62, 63
  of investors, 62
  organizational perspective, 16, 27, 28, 68
  outsider's perspective, 65–70
  thinking beyond oneself, 41–44, *43*
  well-defined point of view needed for CEOs, 97
Peterson, Doug
  biography of, 176
  on early career CEOs, 18, 25, 46, 52, 53
  on middle career CEOs, 62, 76, 78
Plato, 110
politics and organizational culture
  Culture Change (reflection exercise #2), 118–19
  succession planning and, 87
post-CEO portfolio, shaping, 93–96
potential CEO, becoming. *see* CEO leadership cycle, becoming high-potential CEO
Powell, Ken, 26, 62, 177
predecessors. *see* succession of CEOs
primacy effect, 47
prioritizing. *see* time management
Procter & Gamble, 49

"profoundly simple" thinking zone, 114
Publicis, 72–73, 170

Q

questions. *see also* reflection exercises
    Are You Asking the Right Questions?, *43*
    for outsider's perspective, 66–68

R

reflection exercises, 113–37
    #1: Direction Setting, 114–15, *116–17*
    #2: Culture Change, 118–19, *120–21*
    #3: Team Performance, 122–23, *124–25*
    #4: Board Effectiveness, 126–27, *128–29*
    #5: Stakeholder Engagement, 130–31, *132–33*
    #6: Personal Leadership Effectiveness, 134–35, *136–37*
    for all four seasons, 113
relationships. *see* reputation
relay race analogy, 81–82, 96
reputation
    outsider's perspective, 68
    self-assessment of, 31
    stress-testing relationships with stakeholders, 76
responsibility fulfillment, self-assessment for, 12–18, *13–15*
retirement, post-CEO roles and, 93–96
risk aversion, 29
risk identification, 75–77
"road builders" vs. "flag planters," 29

role modeling
    learning from successful CEOs, 6–7
    for talent management, 54
Roosevelt, Franklin D., 107, 122
Rubinstein, Arthur, 3

S

Salesforce, 64
same-sex marriage, 103
Schutz, William, 114
Schwarzman, Stephen, 27, 178
S-curve strategy, 4, 70–74
selection process for CEOs, 33–37
self-assessment by CEOs. *see also* reflection exercises
    for analyzing CEO potential, 30–33
    for learning enhancement, 64
    for post-CEO roles, 93–96
    on responsibility fulfillment vs. blind spots, 12–18, *13–15*
    for timing of departure, 83–85
self-awareness, cultivating, 107–8
Setúbal, Roberto, 69, 71, 179
737 MAX, 74
shareholders
    excess TRS (total financial return to shareholders), 9–10, *11*
    future of CEO role and, 106
shoshin concept, 64
Silverman, Josh, 22, 42, 43–44, 51–52, 61, 180
*Situational Leader, The* (Hersey), 134
Smith, Brad
    biography of, 181
    on humility of aspiring CEOs, 30, 32
    on late career CEOs, 85, 91, 92, 94–95
    on middle career CEOs, 61–64, 69, 77

Smith, Richard, 75
Smith, Robert F., 31, 77, 182
Sony, 84, 163
"sophomore slump," 7
S&P Global, 18, 25, 46, 52, 53, 62, 76, 78. *see also* Peterson, Doug
"spring" cycle of CEOs, 4, 5. *see also* CEO leadership cycle, becoming high-potential CEO
stakeholders. *see also* shareholders
    Direction Setting (reflection exercise #1), 114–15, *116–17*
    Stakeholder Engagement (reflection exercise #5), 130–31, *132–33*
    stepping up to CEO role and perspective of, 27, 28–29
    stress-testing relationships with, 76
Stark, Robert, 7
starting strong in CEO role. *see* CEO leadership cycle, early years
staying ahead as CEO. *see* CEO leadership cycle, mid-tenure years
stepping up to CEO role. *see* CEO leadership cycle, becoming high-potential CEO
strategy questions, for outsider's perspective, 67
stress-testing, 75–76
Strovink, Kurt
    *CEO for All Seasons*, 6–8
    *The Journey of Leadership*, 6
succession of CEOs. *see also* CEO leadership cycle, late-tenure years
    advance planning for, 77–78
    four-season analogy of, 3–5, 105
    internal vs. external hiring, 36–37
    planning for, 86–89

"summer" cycle of CEOs, 4. *see also* CEO leadership cycle, early years
supermarket experiment, 65–66
sustainable mindset, 23–25, *24*

**T**

talent management
    change in workforce trends and, 100–101, 103
    future-proofing, 77–78
    prioritizing, 52–54
    workforce size and, 107
Tan, Lip-Bu, 89, 183
Team Performance (reflection exercise #3), 122–23, *124–25*
technology, expecting change in, 99, 102, 106
Teresa, Saint (Mother Teresa), 126
time management, 52–53, 109
timing decision, for departure, 83–85. *see also* CEO leadership cycle, late-tenure years
Top 30 CEOs *(Barron's)*, 9
Top 100 CEOs *(Harvard Business Review)*, 9
"Tortoise and the Hare, The" (Aesop's fable), 57–58
transition, change vs., 41
transitioning out of CEO role. *see* CEO leadership cycle, late-tenure years
transitioning to CEO role. *see* CEO leadership cycle, becoming high-potential CEO
*Transitions* (Bridges), 41
Truman, Harry, 93
Twain, Mark, 101

**U**

"unfreezing" moment, 40–41
Unibanco, 71

United Airlines, 75
U.S. Bancorp, 49, 78, 148

V

vision of organization
    blind spots of CEOs and, 16
    Direction Setting (reflection exercise #1), 114–15, *116–17*
    vision statement brevity, 46–47
Vista Equity Partners, 31, 77, 182

W

*Wall Street Journal*, 92
Wennink, Peter, 11–12, 25, 26, 48, 64, 95, 184
Westpac, 11, 28, 31, 51, 54, 84, 87, 93, 166. *see also* Kelly, Gail
"why." *see* motivation
"winter" cycle of CEOs, 4, 5. *see also* CEO leadership cycle, late-tenure years
Wirth, Michael, 28, 62, 69, 75, 104, 185
workforce. *see* talent management
World's Most Powerful Women of 2024 *(Forbes)*, 11

X

Xerox, 93

## ABOUT McKINSEY & COMPANY

McKinsey & Company is a global management consulting firm committed to helping organizations accelerate sustainable and inclusive growth. We work with clients across the private, public, and social sectors to solve complex problems and create positive change for all their stakeholders. We have a presence in sixty-seven countries, and our clients represent 80 percent of the Fortune 500 and Global 1000.

McKinsey was founded on the ideal of following a top management approach. As a result, we have a long history of counseling CEOs directly on their biggest and most important challenges and opportunities. We recognize fully that for a company to succeed as an institution, the CEO needs to excel in their role. Further, every year the firm invests more than $700 million in research and analysis, the vast majority of which is on CEO-relevant topics.

Our CEO Excellence practice was created to help CEOs maximize their impact in each of the six responsibilities of their job: setting the strategy, aligning the organization, leading the top team, working with the board, being the face of the company to external stakeholders, and managing their own time and energy. To help them do so, we draw on our proprietary research, insights, and tools while leveraging our experience helping thousands of CEOs.

The toolkit we've developed, which applies to all of the learnings shared in this book and in the *New York Times* bestseller *CEO Excellence: The Six Mindsets That Distinguish the Best Leaders from the Rest*, supports CEOs in achieving excellence through each of the four seasons of their tenure:

**CEO Candidate Preparation:** We partner with executives aspiring to become CEO—ranging from those new to the C-suite to those actively in the running—by helping them understand the role and the journey. We develop their skills and hone their leadership style and personal operating model to help make them a viable candidate able to navigate the selection process. We also work with the CEO and board to establish a rigorous succession-planning process.

**CEO Transition and Onboarding:** We support a new CEO's transition planning—from setting an aspirational strategy and developing a transformation agenda, to formulating the near-term tactics related to organizational alignment, mobilizing the executive team, engaging the board and other stakeholders, and putting in place a robust personal operating model. The approach applies practical and proven playbooks, tools, and insights. We also facilitate learning and networking experiences with experienced CEO mentors to the extent desired.

**Mid-Tenure CEO Excellence:** We help CEOs during their middle years to ensure they aren't getting complacent by bringing new ideas, facilitating unique learning experiences, and objectively taking stock of all aspects of CEO effectiveness and business results. This process effectively identifies a series of performance-improving "S-curves" for both the individual and institution.

*CEO Succession Planning:* We work with the board and incumbent CEO to assess the timing for the transition, build and develop the succession pipeline, orchestrate a seamless transition, and set up the next CEO for success while helping the current CEO to finish strong. We also help prepare the incumbent CEO for their next journey.

To learn more about the support available, please reach out to CEO_Excellence@McKinsey.com.

## ABOUT THE AUTHORS

Carolyn, Scott, and Vik coauthored the *New York Times* bestseller *CEO Excellence*, which filled an important literary void for CEOs aiming to distinguish themselves. For *A CEO for All Seasons*, they were joined by Kurt Strovink, who is the coauthor of McKinsey's most recent book on leadership (*The Journey of Leadership*), also a national bestseller. Collectively, the authors have written many articles that have been featured in the *McKinsey Quarterly*, *Forbes*, *Chief Executive Magazine*, and *Harvard Business Review*. They also regularly give keynote speeches and lectures at MBA schools, host CEO and senior executive roundtables across industries, and serve as faculty for McKinsey's executive programs (The Bower Forum, The CEO Excellence Forum, and Executive Transitions Master Class, among others).

**Carolyn Dewar** is a senior partner in McKinsey & Company's San Francisco office, which she joined in 2000. She is the founder and co-leader of McKinsey's global CEO Excellence service line (with Scott) and a senior leader in the global Strategy & Corporate Finance Practice, Governance Taskforce, and Partner Evaluation Committee. Carolyn advises CEOs and executive teams globally on critical moments of transformation, growth acceleration, mergers and acquisitions, and strategic pivots. Active in her community, she serves on several charitable boards. Having lived and traveled around the world, Carolyn enjoys the nature, culinary adventures, and vibrant culture of her home in Northern California, where she now lives with her husband, Thomas, and their children, Gray and Evening.

**Scott Keller** is a senior partner in McKinsey's Southern California office, having joined McKinsey & Company in 1995. He co-leads (with Carolyn) the firm's global CEO Excellence service line. Beyond serving clients, he has authored seven books in the field of organization effectiveness, including the national bestseller *Beyond Performance*. Outside of McKinsey, he is a co-founder of Digital Divide Data, a multi-award-winning social enterprise. Further afield, Scott is a guitarist, songwriter, and producer and is a featured musician in *Rock Camp: The Movie* (2021). He's also one of a few hundred people known to have traveled to every country in the world. His favorite place, however, is Southern California, where he lives with his wife, Fiona, and his three boys, Lachlan, Jackson, and Camden.

**Vikram (Vik) Malhotra** is a senior partner in McKinsey & Company's New York office who joined the firm in 1986. In addition to serving on McKinsey's Board of Directors as chair of the People Committee and the Governance & Risk Committee, Vik has also served as the Managing Partner of the Americas, led McKinsey's Senior Partner Review Committee and Professional Standards Committee, and represented McKinsey at forums such as The World Economic Forum in Davos. He currently serves on the Advisory Board at the Wharton School of the University of Pennsylvania. He's also a trustee of The New York City Partnership, a trustee emeritus of the Asia Society, and a former trustee of The Conference Board. Vik enjoys traveling and spending time with his wife, Mary, and his children Malu, Devan, and Nik.

## ABOUT THE AUTHORS

**Kurt Strovink** is a senior partner in McKinsey & Company's New York office, having joined the firm in 1996. He leads McKinsey's global CEO practice and serves as a member of McKinsey's Board of Directors and extended Executive Committee. He previously led the firm's global work in the insurance sector, the Strategy & Corporate Finance Practice in the Americas, the Global Client Council, governance modernization for the firm, and the New York office as its managing partner. Over the past twenty years, Kurt has led a number of pro bono efforts in education, including work with Teach for America, where he was formerly on the national board. He is a member of the Board of Trustees and the Executive Committee of the Board of Carnegie Hall. He lives in Scarsdale, New York, with his wife, Lisa, and two sons, Aidan and Christopher.